Practicing Standardized Test Formats

Grade K

aligned with *Reading Mastery*

- Adapts concepts covered in Reading Mastery to address important test concepts and instructional standards
- Familiarizes students with questions and formats from the most recent test forms
- Helps student perform at their optimal level and obtain scores that accurately reflect achievement.

Columbus, OH

Acknowledgements
The publisher would like to thank Michael Milone, Ph.D., Assessment Specialist, for his help in preparing these test practice materials.

SRAonline.com

SRA

Printed in the United States of America.

Send all inquiries to this address:
SRA/McGraw-Hill
8787 Orion Place
Columbus, OH 43240-4027

ISBN: 978-0-07-612242-4
MHID: 0-07-612242-5

8 9 10 11 12 GPC 20 19 18 17

The McGraw·Hill Companies

Table of Contents

Introduction

The *Practicing Standardized Test Formats* supplement to *Reading Mastery Signature Edition* engages your students in activities that will prepare them to succeed on state and standardized tests. The activities are based on the content of *Reading Mastery,* the assessment format of various tests, and widely accepted standards for assessment.

When students apply the skills they have learned on a regular basis, they develop the automaticity and confidence needed to succeed on formal assessments. They are more comfortable when they take a test and, as a result, their performance on the test is a more accurate reflection of their true abilities. Providing frequent practice with feedback enhances students' reading and test-taking skills in a number of ways. Students are more likely to

- read for understanding
- follow directions correctly
- avoid common mistakes
- recognize item formats
- understand the language of assessment

Throughout this supplement, students will apply the concepts covered in *Reading Mastery* to a standardized test format. Although the test format varies by grade level, most of the items are multiple choice. In Grade 1 and higher, students will occasionally respond by writing a short extended answer, a response format featured on many contemporary assessments.

The majority of the assessments are based on the instruction and practice featured in *Reading Mastery.* Periodically, students will be expected to respond to new content selections that they listen to or read independently. This balance of familiar and novel content is intended to maintain students' comfort level while introducing them to more challenging material.

In Grades K and 1, you administer all the items orally. This practice builds students' listening skills and familiarizes them with test-taking procedures. In Grades 2 and higher, you may administer the assessments orally or independently. In all cases, be sure to familiarize students with words or assessment constructions that are unfamiliar to them. In addition, encourage your students to use general test-taking strategies such as listening carefully, taking the best guess, and using the process of elimination. Explain the correct answers and discuss how the correct answers can be found.

The following guidelines will help you decide how to administer the assessment:

- For students who are not yet reading independently, consider reading all of the assessments aloud while they follow along. Have them answer each question on their own immediately after it is read aloud.
- For students who can read some of the content independently, preread the entire assessment to them. Ask students to complete the assessment independently. Be available to provide any assistance they may need.
- For students who can read with at least moderate independence, allow them to complete the assessment on their own. Be available to provide any assistance they may need.

In all cases, review the assessments with students as soon as they have completed them. Explain the correct answers and discuss how the correct answers can be found, demonstrating appropriate test-taking strategies. Clarify any misunderstandings students have about answering the questions, not assuming that they understand how to answer them. As part of the review, use a "think-aloud" approach to model how to find answers. Modeling these solutions is the most dependable way to teach metacognitive test-taking strategies.

Lesson 21

(Duplicate the test page for each child and fill in the name and date on each test. Be sure each child has a pencil. Distribute the tests.)

1 **(Hold up the test page. Touch the beginning of row 1.)** Today we are going to practice answering different kinds of questions. We will do the questions together. Put your finger on row 1. **(Check to be sure the students have found the correct row of answers.)** There is a little bubble under each answer in row 1. **(Point out the three pictures with bubbles beneath.)** I'm going to ask you a question. When you know the answer, use your pencil to fill in the bubble under the right answer. Listen carefully. Here's the first question. Look at the pictures. Which picture shows an airplane? **(Hold up the test page, and model filling in the third bubble.)** I fill in the third bubble because this is the answer that shows an airplane. Now use your pencil to fill in the right answer. **(Allow time for students to find the correct answer and fill it in. Check to make sure all students are following directions.)**

2 Let's do another one. Touch row 2. **(Check to be sure the students have found the correct row of answers.)** Here's the question. Listen carefully. Look at the pictures. **(Point out the three pictures.)** Which answer shows something you can eat? **(Hold up the test page, and model filling in the first bubble.)** I fill in the first bubble because this is the answer that shows something you can eat. Now use your pencil to fill in the right answer. **(Allow time for students to find the correct answer and fill it in. Check to make sure all students are following directions.)**

3 Touch row 3. **(Check to be sure the students have found the correct row of answers.)** Here's the next question. Look at the letters. **(Point out the three letters.)** Which answer shows the letter that makes the sound **aaa? (Hold up the test page, and model filling in the second bubble.)** I fill in the second bubble because this is the letter that makes the sound **aaa.** Now use your pencil to fill in the right answer. **(Allow time for students to find the correct answer and fill it in. Check to make sure all students are following directions.)**

4 Touch row 4. **(Check to be sure the students have found the correct row of answers.)** Here's the question. Look at the pictures. **(Point out the three pictures.)** Which answer shows a sock? **(Hold up the test page, and model filling in the first bubble.)** I fill in the first bubble because this is a picture of a sock. Now use your pencil to fill in the right answer. **(Allow time for students to find the correct answer and fill it in. Check to make sure all students are following directions.)**

It's time to stop. You did a good job filling in the bubbles. Let's go over your answers. **(Review the answers with the children. Collect the test pages.)**

Lesson 21

Name ______________________ Date ______________

1

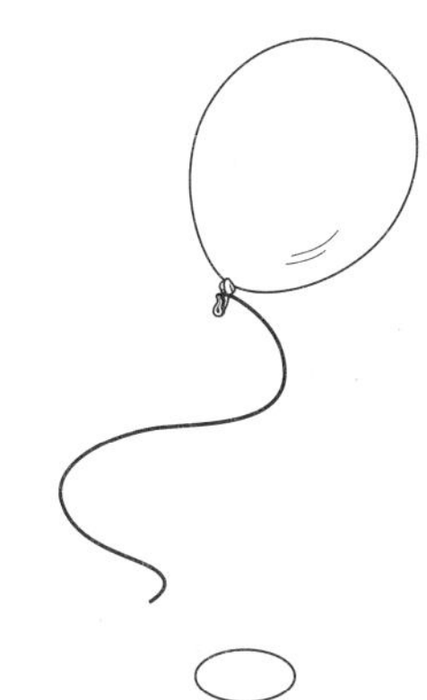

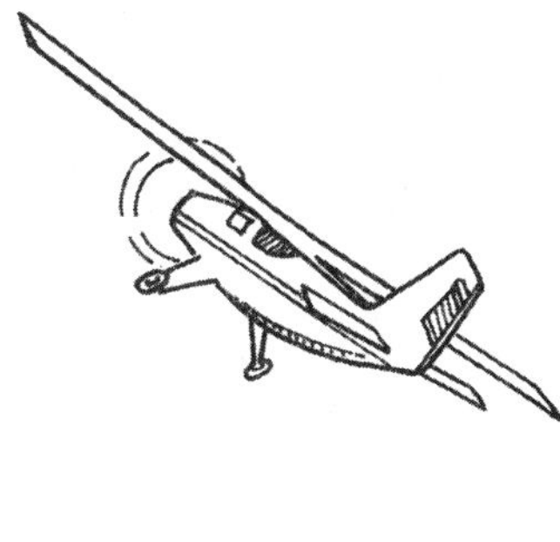

2

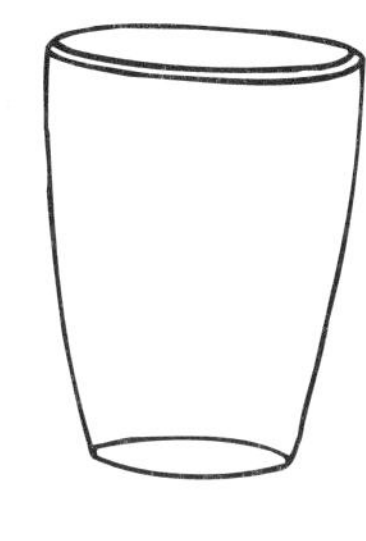

3

s

v

4

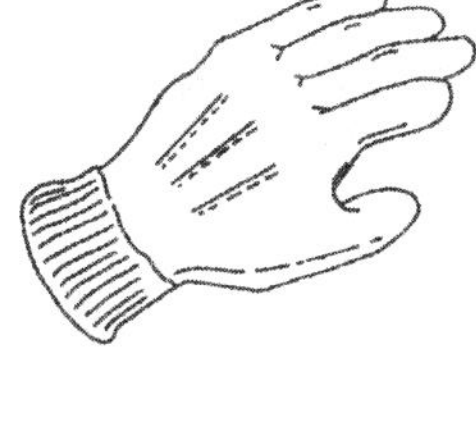

Lesson 22

(Duplicate the test page for each child and fill in the name and date on each test. Be sure each child has a pencil. Distribute the tests.)

1. (Hold up the test page. Touch the beginning of row 1.) Today we are going to practice answering more questions. We will do the first question together. Put your finger on row 1. (Check to be sure the students have found the correct row of answers.) There is a little bubble under each answer in row 1. (Point out the three pictures with bubbles beneath.) I'm going to ask you a question. When you know the answer, use your pencil to fill in the bubble under the right answer. Listen carefully. Here's the first question. Look at the pictures. They show a book, a ring, and a lamp. Which picture begins with the sound **rrr?** (Hold up the test page, and model filling in the second bubble.) I fill in the second bubble because *ring* begins with the sound **rrr.** Now use your pencil to fill in the right answer. (Allow time for students to find the correct answer and fill it in. Check to make sure all students are following directions.)

2. You will answer the rest of the questions yourself. Touch row 2. Here's the question. Listen carefully. Look at the pictures. Which answer shows something you can open? Fill in the space under the answer that shows something you can open. (Allow time for the students to fill in their answers.) You should have filled in the third bubble. If you did not, cross out your answer and fill in the third bubble now.

3. Touch row 3. Here's the next question. Look at the letters. Which answer shows the letter that makes the sound **ēēē?** Fill in the bubble under the letter that makes the sound **ēēē.** (Allow time for the students to fill in their answers.) You should have filled in the first bubble. If you did not, cross out your answer and fill in the first bubble now.

4. Touch row 4. Listen carefully and look at the pictures. They show a net, a rat, and a log. Which picture has the middle sound **aaa?** Fill in the bubble under the picture that has the middle sound **aaa.** (Allow time for the students to fill in their answers.) You should have filled in the second bubble. If you did not, cross out your answer and fill in the second bubble now.

It's time to stop. You did a good job filling in the bubbles. Let's go over your answers. **(Review the answers with the children. Collect the test pages.)**

Lesson 22

Name ______________________ Date ______________

1

2

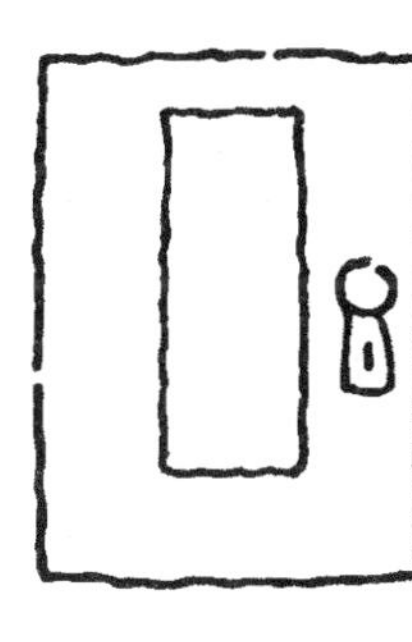

3

e s w

4

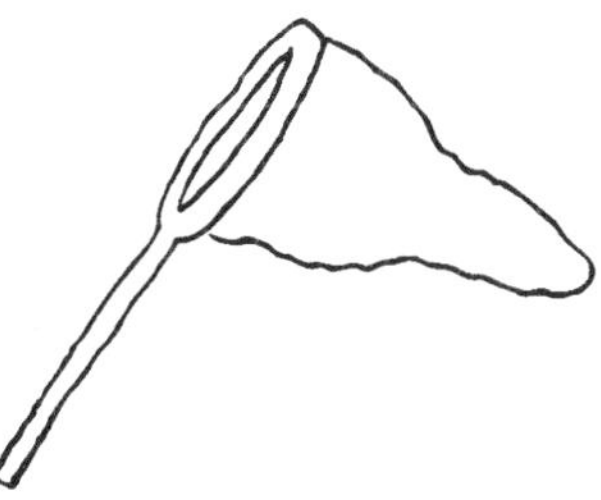

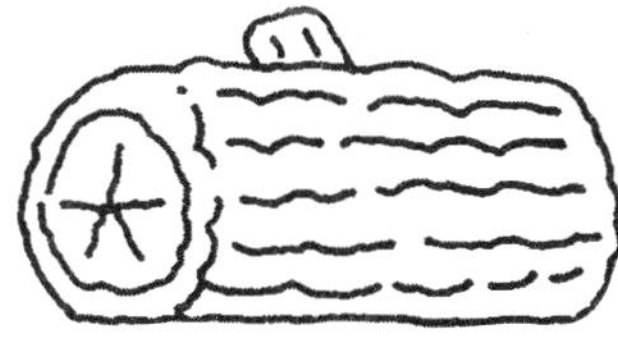

Lesson 23

(Duplicate the test page for each child and fill in the name and date on each test. Be sure each child has a pencil. Distribute the tests.)

1 (Hold up the test page. Touch the beginning of row 1.) Today we are going to practice answering more questions. We will do the first question together. Put your finger on row 1. (Check to be sure the students have found the correct row of answers.) There is a little bubble under each answer in row 1. (Point out the three pictures with bubbles beneath.) I'm going to ask you a question. When you know the answer, use your pencil to fill in the bubble under the right answer. Listen carefully. Here's the first question. Look at the pictures. They show a fan, a pan, and a man. Which picture begins with the sound **fff?** (Hold up the test page, and model filling in the first bubble.) I fill in the first bubble because *fan* begins with the sound **fff.** Now use your pencil to fill in the right answer. (Allow time for students to find the correct answer and fill it in. Check to make sure all students are following directions.)

2 You will answer the rest of the questions yourself. Touch row 2. Here's the question. Listen carefully and look at the pictures. Which answer shows a girl in the rain? Fill in the bubble under the answer that shows a girl in the rain. (Allow time for the students to fill in their answers.) You should have filled in the second bubble. If you did not, cross out your answer and fill in the second bubble now.

3 Touch row 3. Here's the next question. Look at the letters. Which answer shows the letter that makes the sound **mmm?** Fill in the bubble under the letter that makes the sound **mmm.** (Allow time for the students to fill in their answers.) You should have filled in the first bubble. If you did not, cross out your answer and fill in the first bubble now.

4 Touch row 4. Here's the question. Look at the pictures. They show a pot, a van, and a leaf. Which picture has the middle sound **ēēē?** Fill in the bubble under the picture that has the middle sound **ēēē.** (Allow time for the students to fill in their answers.) You should have filled in the third bubble. If you did not, cross out your answer and fill in the third bubble now.

It's time to stop. You did a good job filling in the bubbles. Let's go over your answers. **(Review the answers with the children. Collect the test pages.)**

Lesson 23

Name ______________________ Date ______________

1

2

3

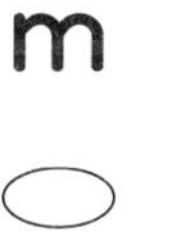

s

4

Lesson 24

(Duplicate the test page for each child and fill in the name and date on each test. Be sure each child has a pencil. Distribute the tests.)

1. (Hold up the test page. Touch the beginning of row 1.) Today we are going to practice answering more questions. We will do the first question together. Put your finger on row 1. (Check to be sure the students have found the correct row of answers.) There is a little bubble under each answer in row 1. (Point out the three pictures with bubbles beneath.) I'm going to ask you a question. When you know the answer, use your pencil to fill in the bubble under the right answer. Listen carefully. Here's the first question. Look at the pictures. They show a dog, the sun, and a boat. Which picture begins with the sound **sss?** (Hold up the test page, and model filling in the second bubble.) I fill in the second bubble because *sun* begins with the sound **sss.** Now use your pencil to fill in the right answer. (Allow time for students to find the correct answer and fill it in. Check to make sure all students are following directions.)

2. You will answer the rest of the questions yourself. Touch row 2. Here's the question. Listen carefully. Look at the pictures. Which answer shows a rope? Fill in the bubble under the answer that shows a rope. (Allow time for the students to fill in their answers.) You should have filled in the third bubble. If you did not, cross out your answer and fill in the third bubble now.

3. Touch row 3. Here's the next question. Look at the letters. Which answer shows the letter that makes the sound **rrr?** Fill in the bubble under the letter that makes the sound **rrr.** (Allow time for the students to fill in their answers.) You should have filled in the first bubble. If you did not, cross out your answer and fill in the first bubble now.

4. Touch row 4. Here's the question. Listen carefully and look at the answers. Which answer shows the letters that make the sounds **mmm ēēē?** Fill in the bubble under the letters that make the sounds **mmm ēēē.** (Allow time for the students to fill in their answers.) You should have filled in the second bubble. If you did not, cross out your answer and fill in the second bubble now.

It's time to stop. You did a good job filling in the bubbles. Let's go over your answers. **(Review the answers with the children. Collect the test pages.)**

Lesson 24

Name ____________________ Date ____________

1

2

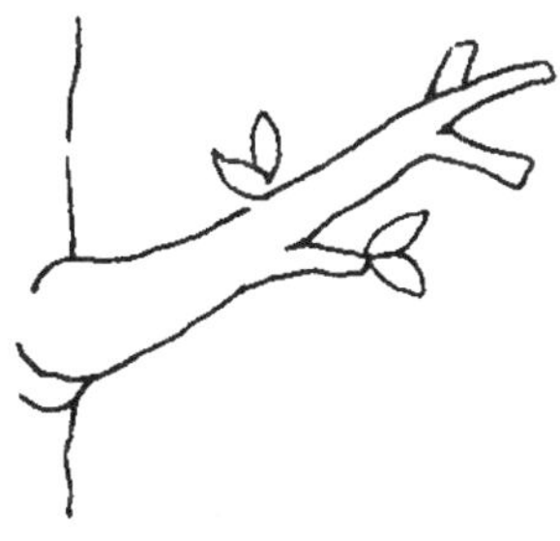

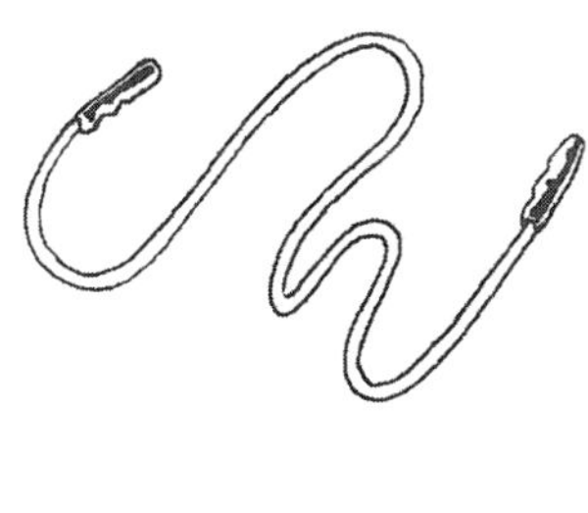

3 r s a

4 am me er

Lesson 25

(Duplicate the test page for each child and fill in the name and date on each test. Be sure each child has a pencil. Distribute the tests.)

1 (Hold up the test page. Touch the beginning of row 1.) Today we are going to practice answering more questions. We will do the first question together. Put your finger on row 1. (Check to be sure the students have found the correct row of answers.) There is a little bubble under each answer in row 1. (Point out the three pictures with bubbles beneath.) I'm going to ask you a question. When you know the answer, use your pencil to fill in the bubble under the right answer. Listen carefully. Here's the first question. Look at the pictures. They show a fish, a mop, and a sack. Which picture has the sound **aaa** in the middle? (Hold up the test page, and model filling in the third bubble.) I fill in the third bubble because *sack* has the middle sound **aaa.** Now use your pencil to fill in the right answer. (Allow time for students to find the correct answer and fill it in. Check to make sure all students are following directions.)

2 You will answer the rest of the questions yourself. Touch row 2. Here's the question. Listen carefully. Look at the pictures. They show a comb, a bike, and a nail. Which answer shows something you can ride? Fill in the bubble under the answer that shows something you can ride. (Allow time for the students to fill in their answers.) You should have filled in the second bubble. If you did not, cross out your answer and fill in the second bubble now.

3 Touch row 3. Here's the next question. Look at the letters. Which answer shows the letter that makes the sound **sss?** Fill in the bubble under the letter that makes the sound **sss.** (Allow time for the students to fill in their answers.) You should have filled in the first bubble. If you did not, cross out your answer and fill in the first bubble now.

4 Touch row 4. Here's the question. Listen carefully and look at the answers. Which answer shows the letters that make the sounds **rrr ēēē?** Fill in the bubble under the letters that make the sounds **rrr ēēē.** (Allow time for the students to fill in their answers.) You should have filled in the third bubble. If you did not, cross out your answer and fill in the third bubble now.

It's time to stop. You did a good job filling in the bubbles. Let's go over your answers. **(Review the answers with the children. Collect the test pages.)**

Lesson 25

Name ______________________ Date ______________

1

2

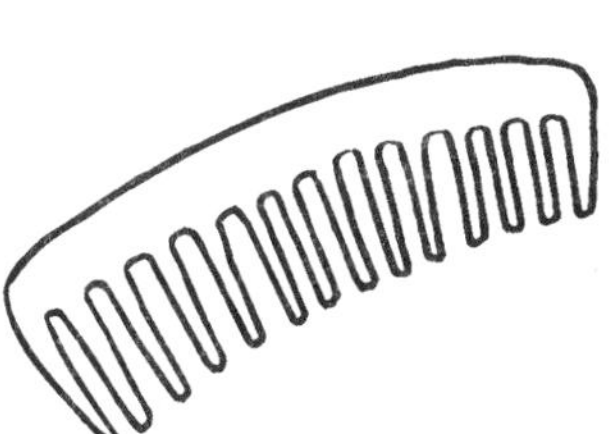

3

s　　a　　r

4

r s　　a r　　r e

Lesson 26

(Duplicate the test page for each child and fill in the name and date on each test. Be sure each child has a pencil. Distribute the tests.)

1. Put your finger on row 1. Look at the pictures. Which picture shows an **ear?** Fill in the bubble under the picture of the **ear.** (Allow time for the students to fill in their answers.) You should have filled in the second bubble. If you did not, cross out your answer and fill in the second bubble now.

2. Touch row 2. Look at the answers. Two of the answers are the same, and one is different. Which answer is different? Fill in the bubble under the answer that is different. (Allow time for the students to fill in their answers.) You should have filled in the second bubble. If you did not, cross out your answer and fill in the second bubble now.

3. Touch row 3. Look at the pictures. They show a car, a plane, and a boat. Which picture ends with **rrr?** Fill in the bubble under the picture that ends with **rrr.** (Allow time for the students to fill in their answers.) You should have filled in the first bubble. If you did not, cross out your answer and fill in the first bubble now.

4. Touch row 4. Look at the pictures. They show a pan, a hat, and a deer. Which answer has a different middle sound from the others? Fill in the bubble under the picture that has a different middle sound. (Allow time for the students to fill in their answers.) You should have filled in the third bubble. If you did not, cross out your answer and fill in the third bubble now.

It's time to stop. You did a good job filling in the bubbles. Let's go over your answers. **(Review the answers with the children. Collect the test pages.)**

Lesson 26

Name ______________________ Date ____________

1

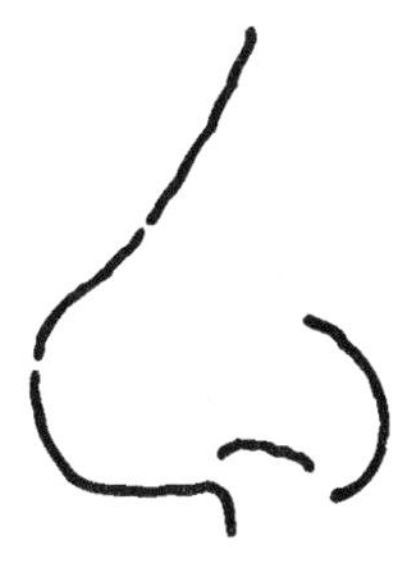

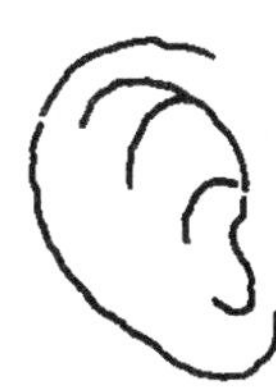

○ ○ ○

2

m

a

○ ○ ○

3

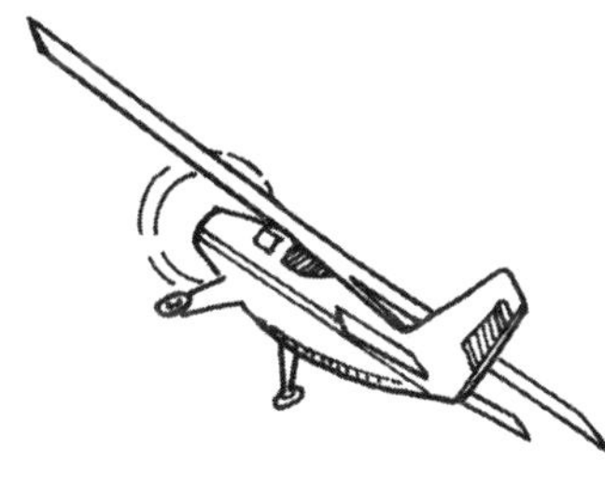

○ ○ ○

4

○ ○ ○

Lesson 27

(Duplicate the test page for each child and fill in the name and date on each test. Be sure each child has a pencil. Distribute the tests.)

1. Put your finger on row 1. Look at the pictures. Which answer shows a picture that ends with the sound **eat?** Fill in the bubble under the picture that ends like **eat.** (Allow time for the students to fill in their answers.) You should have filled in the third bubble. If you did not, cross out your answer and fill in the third bubble now.

2. Touch row 2. Look at the pictures. They show a fork, a watch, and a box. Which answer is something you use to eat? Fill in the bubble under the picture of something you use to eat. (Allow time for the students to fill in their answers.) You should have filled in the first bubble. If you did not, cross out your answer and fill in the first bubble now.

3. Touch row 3. Here's the next question. Look at the letters. Which answer shows the letter that makes the sound **d?** Fill in the bubble under the letter that makes the sound **d.** (Allow time for the students to fill in their answers.) You should have filled in the second bubble. If you did not, cross out your answer and fill in the second bubble now.

4. Touch row 3. Look at the pictures. They show an arm, a shell, and a bell. Which picture ends with **mmm?** Fill in the bubble under the picture that ends with **mmm.** (Allow time for the students to fill in their answers.) You should have filled in the first bubble. If you did not, cross out your answer and fill in the first bubble now.

It's time to stop. You did a good job filling in the bubbles. Let's go over your answers. **(Review the answers with the children. Collect the test pages.)**

Lesson 27

Name ______________________ Date ______________

1

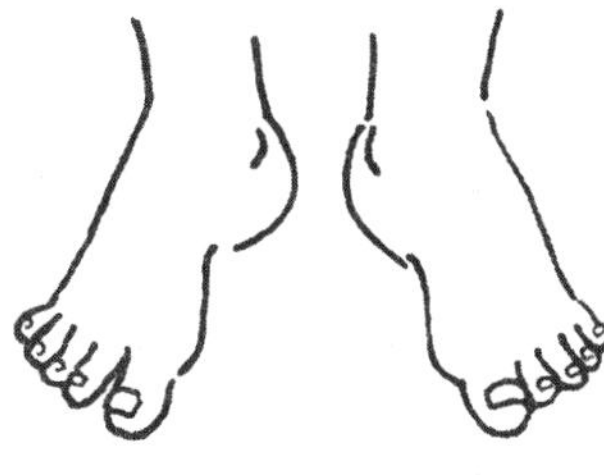

2

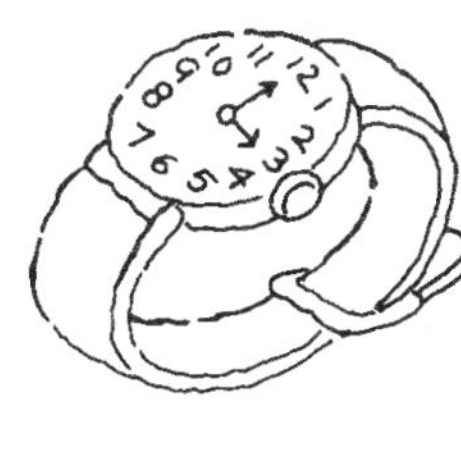

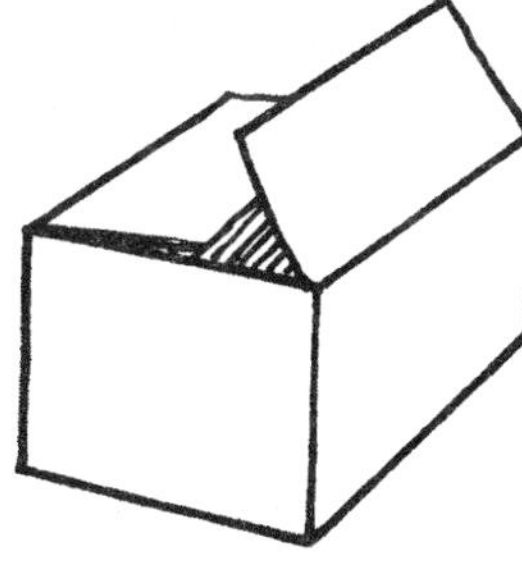

3

r d a

4

(Duplicate the test page for each child and fill in the name and date on each test. Be sure each child has a pencil. Distribute the tests.)

1. Put your finger on row 1. Look at the pictures. They show a bus, a bed, and a bike. Which one ends with the sound **d?** Fill in the bubble under the picture that ends with the sound **d.** (Allow time for the students to fill in their answers.) You should have filled in the second bubble. If you did not, cross out your answer and fill in the second bubble now.

2. Touch row 2. Look at the answers. Which answer shows **aaa mmm?** Fill in the bubble under the answer that shows **aaa mmm.** (Allow time for the students to fill in their answers.) You should have filled in the first bubble. If you did not, cross out your answer and fill in the first bubble now.

3. Touch row 3. Look at the letters. Two answers are the same and one is different. Which answer is different? Fill in the bubble under the answer that is different. (Allow time for the students to fill in their answers.) You should have filled in the third bubble. If you did not, cross out your answer and fill in the third bubble now.

4. Touch row 4. Look at the pictures. Which answer shows a man? Fill in the bubble under the man. (Allow time for the students to fill in their answers.) You should have filled in the second bubble. If you did not, cross out your answer and fill in the second bubble now.

It's time to stop. You did a good job filling in the bubbles. Let's go over your answers. **(Review the answers with the children. Collect the test pages.)**

Lesson 28

Name ______________________ Date ______________

1

2

am er sa

3

ee ee me

4

Lesson 29

(Duplicate the test page for each child and fill in the name and date on each test. Be sure each child has a pencil. Distribute the tests.)

1. Put your finger on row 1. Look at the pictures. Which one is soap? Fill in the bubble under the picture of the soap. (Allow time for the students to fill in their answers.) You should have filled in the third bubble. If you did not, cross out your answer and fill in the third bubble now.

2. Touch row 2. Look at the pictures. Which answer shows a picture that ends with the sound **ock?** Fill in the bubble under the picture that ends like **ock.** (Allow time for the students to fill in their answers.) You should have filled in the second bubble. If you did not, cross out your answer and fill in the second bubble now.

3. Touch row 3. Look at the pictures. They show an apple, an onion, and an egg. Which picture begins with **aaa?** Fill in the bubble under the picture of something that begins with **aaa.** (Allow time for the students to fill in their answers.) You should have filled in the first bubble. If you did not, cross out your answer and fill in the first bubble now.

4. Touch row 4. Look at the pictures. They show a nail, a fan, and a star. Which picture ends with the sound **an?** Fill in the bubble under the picture of something that ends like **an.** (Allow time for the students to fill in their answers.) You should have filled in the second bubble. If you did not, cross out your answer and fill in the second bubble now.

It's time to stop. You did a good job filling in the bubbles. Let's go over your answers. **(Review the answers with the children. Collect the test pages.)**

Lesson 29

Name ______________________ Date ______________

1

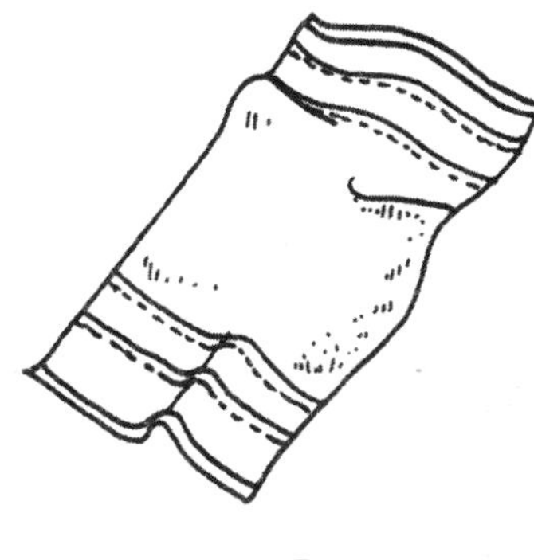

2

3

4

Lesson 30

(Duplicate the test page for each child and fill in the name and date on each test. Be sure each child has a pencil. Distribute the tests.)

1 Put your finger on row 1. Look at the pictures. They show a pig, a worm, and a fly. Which picture rhymes with **my?** Fill in the bubble under the picture that rhymes with **my.** (Allow time for the students to fill in their answers.) You should have filled in the third bubble. If you did not, cross out your answer and fill in the third bubble now.

2 Touch row 2. Look at the pictures. Which one shows something you read? Fill in the bubble under something you read. (Allow time for the students to fill in their answers.) You should have filled in the second bubble. If you did not, cross out your answer and fill in the second bubble now.

3 Touch row 3. Look at the letters. Which sound do you hear at the beginning of the word **make?** Fill in the bubble under the sound you hear at the begining of **make?** (Allow time for the students to fill in their answers.) You should have filled in the first bubble. If you did not, cross out your answer and fill in the first bubble now.

4 Touch row 4. Look at the pictures. They show a car, a truck, and a bus. Which picture ends with **sss?** Fill in the bubble under the picture of something that ends with the sound **sss.** (Allow time for the students to fill in their answers.) You should have filled in the third bubble. If you did not, cross out your answer and fill in the third bubble now.

It's time to stop. You did a good job filling in the bubbles. Let's go over your answers. **(Review the answers with the children. Collect the test pages.)**

Lesson 30

Name ______________________ Date ______________

1

2

3

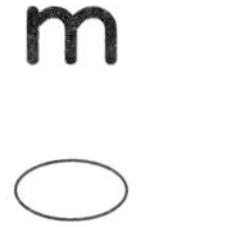

m r s

4

Lesson 31

(Duplicate the test page for each child and fill in the name and date on each test. Be sure each child has a pencil. Distribute the tests.)

1. Put your finger on row 1. Look at the pictures. They show a net, a bat, and a cup. Which picture begins with the sound **nnn?** Fill in the bubble under the picture that begins with **nnn. (Allow time for the students to fill in their answers.)** You should have filled in the first bubble. If you did not, cross out your answer and fill in the first bubble now.

2. Touch row 2. Look at the letters. Which answer shows the letter that makes the sound **fff?** Fill in the bubble under the letter that makes the sound **fff. (Allow time for the students to fill in their answers.)** You should have filled in the third bubble. If you did not, cross out your answer and fill in the third bubble now.

3. Touch row 3. Look at the pictures. They show a door, a clock, and a vest. Which picture ends with **rrr?** Fill in the bubble under the picture that ends with **rrr. (Allow time for the students to fill in their answers.)** You should have filled in the first bubble. If you did not, cross out your answer and fill in the first bubble now.

4. Touch row 4. Look at the pictures. They show a bear, a ram, and a cow. Which picture rhymes with **am?** Fill in the bubble under the picture that rhymes with **am. (Allow time for the students to fill in their answers.)** You should have filled in the second bubble. If you did not, cross out your answer and fill in the second bubble now.

It's time to stop. You did a good job filling in the bubbles. Let's go over your answers. **(Review the answers with the children. Collect the test pages.)**

Lesson 31

Name ______________________ Date ______________

1

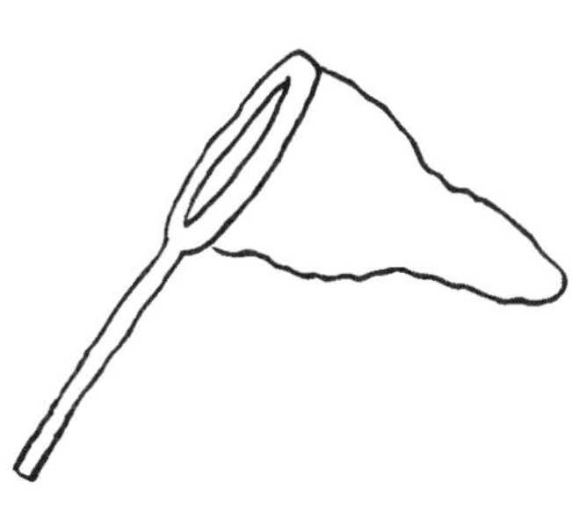

2

d r f

3

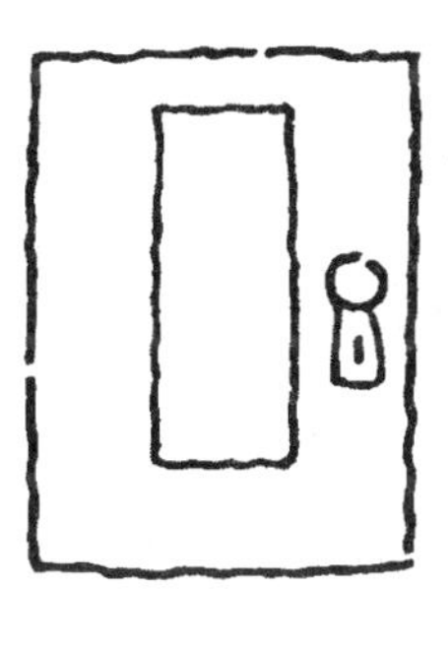

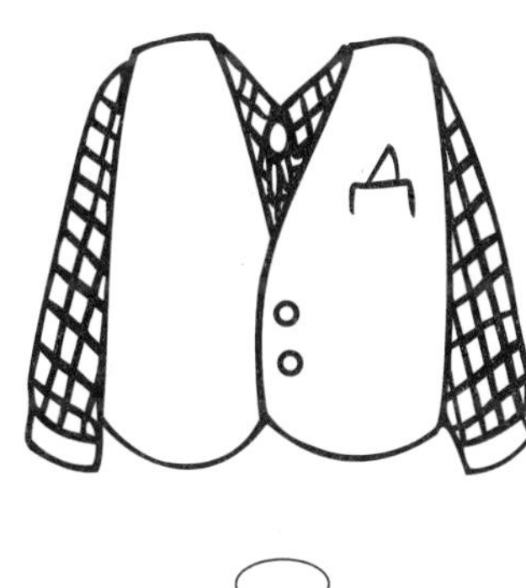

4

(Duplicate the test page for each child and fill in the name and date on each test. Be sure each child has a pencil. Distribute the tests.)

1. Put your finger on row 1. Look at the pictures. They show a bat, a leaf, and a pen. Which picture rhymes with **rat?** Fill in the bubble under the picture that rhymes with **rat.** (Allow time for the students to fill in their answers.) You should have filled in the first bubble. If you did not, cross out your answer and fill in the first bubble now.

2. Touch row 2. Look at the pictures. They show a stamp, a shirt, and a roof. Which picture ends with **fff?** Fill in the bubble under the picture that ends with **fff.** (Allow time for the students to fill in their answers.) You should have filled in the third bubble. If you did not, cross out your answer and fill in the third bubble now.

3. Touch row 3. Look at the pictures. They show a plane, a boat, and a truck. Which picture has the same middle sound as **home?** Fill in the bubble under the picture that has the same middle sound as **home.** (Allow time for the students to fill in their answers.) You should have filled in the second bubble. If you did not, cross out your answer and fill in the second bubble now.

4. Touch row 4. Look at the answers. Which answer is the word **mad?** Fill in the bubble under the word **mad.** (Allow time for the students to fill in their answers.) You should have filled in the first bubble. If you did not, cross out your answer and fill in the first bubble now.

It's time to stop. You did a good job filling in the bubbles. Let's go over your answers. **(Review the answers with the children. Collect the test pages.)**

Name ______________________ Date ______________

1

○ ○ ○

2

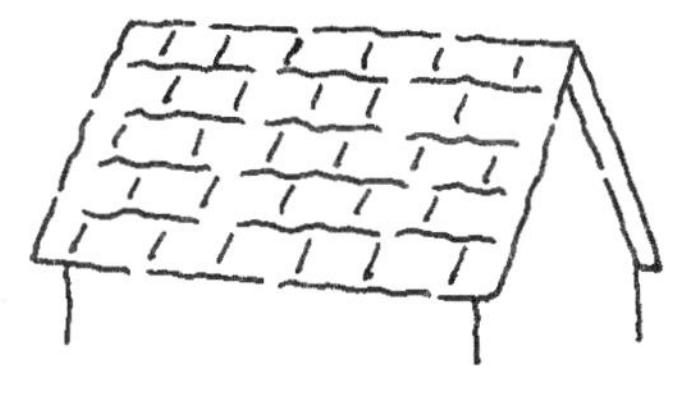

○ ○ ○

3

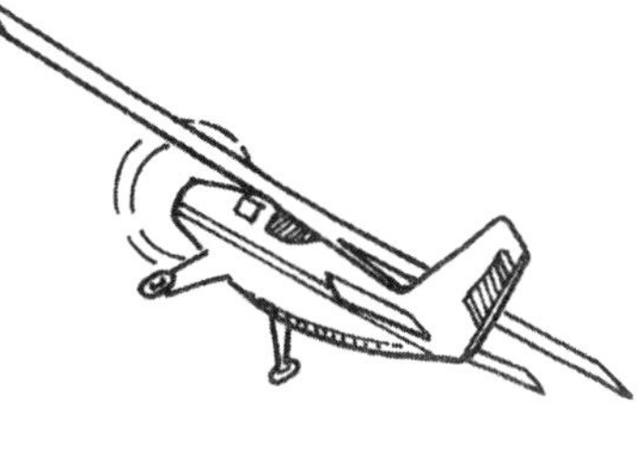

○ ○ ○

4

mad ○

ram ○

mar ○

Lesson 33

(Duplicate the test page for each child and fill in the name and date on each test. Be sure each child has a pencil. Distribute the tests.)

1. Put your finger on row 1. Look at the pictures. They show a cloud, a pail, and a bow. Which picture rhymes with **go?** Fill in the bubble under the picture that rhymes with **go.** (Allow time for the students to fill in their answers.) You should have filled in the third bubble. If you did not, cross out your answer and fill in the third bubble now.

2. Touch row 2. Look at the letters. Which letter makes the sound **rrr?** Fill in the bubble under the letter that makes the sound **rrr.** (Allow time for the students to fill in their answers.) You should have filled in the first bubble. If you did not, cross out your answer and fill in the first bubble now.

3. Touch row 3. Look at the pictures. They show a toe, a boy, and a bee. Which answer ends with the same sound as **see?** Fill in the bubble under the answer that ends with the same sound as **see.** (Allow time for the students to fill in their answers.) You should have filled in the third bubble. If you did not, cross out your answer and fill in the third bubble now.

4. Touch row 4. Look at the answers. Which answer is the word **ear?** Fill in the bubble under the word **ear.** (Allow time for the students to fill in their answers.) You should have filled in the second bubble. If you did not, cross out your answer and fill in the second bubble now.

It's time to stop. You did a good job filling in the bubbles. Let's go over your answers. **(Review the answers with the children. Collect the test pages.)**

Lesson 33

Name ______________________ Date ______________

1

◯ ◯ ◯

2

r ◯

m ◯

d ◯

3

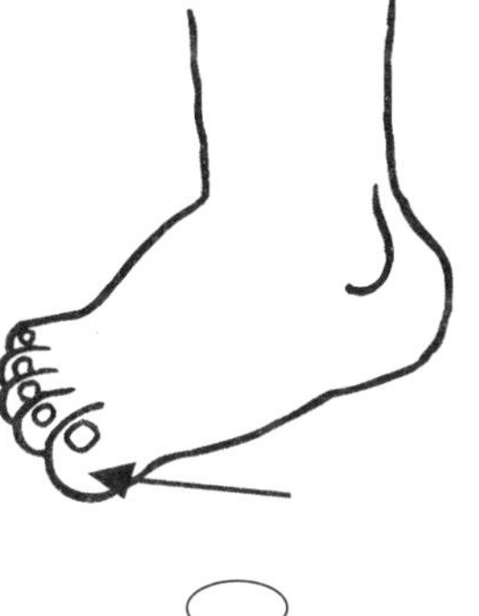

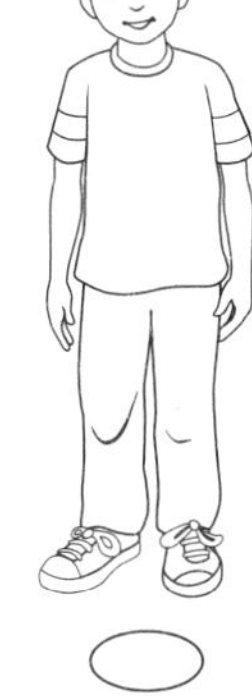

◯ ◯ ◯

4

oak ◯

ear ◯

fan ◯

Lesson 34

(Duplicate the test page for each child and fill in the name and date on each test. Be sure each child has a pencil. Distribute the tests.)

1. Put your finger on row 1. Look at the pictures. They show a dish, a can, and a glass. Which picture rhymes with **fan?** Fill in the bubble under the picture that rhymes with **fan.** (Allow time for the students to fill in their answers.) You should have filled in the second bubble. If you did not, cross out your answer and fill in the second bubble now.

2. Touch row 2. Look at the letters. Which letter makes the sound **iii?** Fill in the bubble under the letter that makes the sound **iii.** (Allow time for the students to fill in their answers.) You should have filled in the first bubble. If you did not, cross out your answer and fill in the first bubble now.

3. Touch row 3. Look at the pictures. They show a bowl, a pan, and a cake. Which answer begins with the same sound as **car?** Fill in the bubble under the answer that begins with the same sound as **car.** (Allow time for the students to fill in their answers.) You should have filled in the third bubble. If you did not, cross out your answer and fill in the third bubble now.

4. Touch row 4. Look at the answers. Which answer is the word **feed?** Fill in the bubble under the word **feed.** (Allow time for the students to fill in their answers.) You should have filled in the third bubble. If you did not, cross out your answer and fill in the third bubble now.

It's time to stop. You did a good job filling in the bubbles. Let's go over your answers.
(Review the answers with the children. Collect the test pages.)

Lesson 34

Name ______________________ Date ______________

1

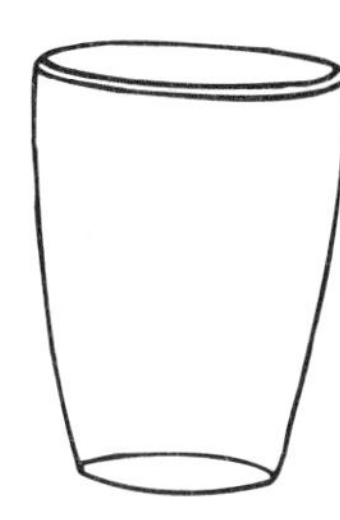

2

i

s

a

3

4

seem

dear

feed

(Duplicate the test page for each child and fill in the name and date on each test. Be sure each child has a pencil. Distribute the tests.)

1. Put your finger on row 1. Look at the letters. Which letter makes the first sound you hear in the word **ink?** Fill in the bubble under the letter that makes the first sound in the word **ink.** (Allow time for the students to fill in their answers.) You should have filled in the second bubble. If you did not, cross out your answer and fill in the second bubble now.

2. Touch row 2. Look at the pictures. They show a pin, a bed, and a cat. Which picture has the same middle sound as **bit?** Fill in the bubble under the picture that has the same middle sound as **bit.** (Allow time for the students to fill in their answers.) You should have filled in the first bubble. If you did not, cross out your answer and fill in the first bubble now.

3. Touch row 3. Look at the pictures. They show a girl, a sack, and a fox. Which picture rhymes with **back?** Fill in the bubble under the picture that rhymes with **back.** (Allow time for the students to fill in their answers.) You should have filled in the second bubble. If you did not, cross out your answer and fill in the second bubble now.

4. Touch row 4. Look at the answers. Which answer is the word **seem?** Fill in the bubble under the word **seem.** (Allow time for the students to fill in their answers.) You should have filled in the third bubble. If you did not, cross out your answer and fill in the third bubble now.

It's time to stop. You did a good job filling in the bubbles. Let's go over your answers. **(Review the answers with the children. Collect the test pages.)**

Lesson 35

Name ______________________ Date ______________

1 a i e

2   

3   

4 rams made seem

Lesson 36

(Duplicate the test page for each child and fill in the name and date on each test. Be sure each child has a pencil. Distribute the tests.)

1. Put your finger on row 1. Look at the pictures. Which picture goes with the words *feed the dog?* Fill in the bubble under the picture that goes with the words *feed the dog.* (Allow time for the students to fill in their answers.) You should have filled in the first bubble. If you did not, cross out your answer and fill in the first bubble now.

2. Touch row 2. Look at the letters. Which letter makes the sound at the end of the word **him?** Fill in the bubble under the letter that makes the sound at the end of the word **him.** (Allow time for the students to fill in their answers.) You should have filled in the second bubble. If you did not, cross out your answer and fill in the second bubble now.

3. Touch row 3. Look at the letters. Which letter makes the first sound in **fun?** Fill in the bubble under the letter that makes the first sound in **fun.** (Allow time for the students to fill in their answers.) You should have filled in the first bubble. If you did not, cross out your answer and fill in the first bubble now.

4. Touch row 4. Look at the answers. Which answer is the word **read?** Fill in the bubble under the word **read.** (Allow time for the students to fill in their answers.) You should have filled in the third bubble. If you did not, cross out your answer and fill in the third bubble now.

It's time to stop. You did a good job filling in the bubbles. Let's go over your answers. **(Review the answers with the children. Collect the test pages.)**

Lesson 36

Name ____________________ Date ____________

1

2 r m d

3 f e s

4 seem fear read

(Duplicate the test page for each child and fill in the name and date on each test. Be sure each child has a pencil. Distribute the tests.)

1 Put your finger on row 1. Look at the letters. Which letter makes the middle sound you hear in the word **seed?** Fill in the bubble under the letter that makes the middle sound in the word **seed.** (Allow time for the students to fill in their answers.) You should have filled in the second bubble. If you did not, cross out your answer and fill in the second bubble now.

2 Touch row 2. Look at the pictures. They show a bird, a fish, and a deer. Which picture rhymes with **fear?** Fill in the bubble under the picture that rhymes with **fear.** (Allow time for the students to fill in their answers.) You should have filled in the third bubble. If you did not, cross out your answer and fill in the third bubble now.

3 Touch row 3. Look at the words. Two of the words are the same and one is different. Which word is different? Fill in the bubble under the word that is different. (Allow time for the students to fill in their answers.) You should have filled in the third bubble. If you did not, cross out your answer and fill in the third bubble now.

4 Touch row 4. Look at the answers. Which answer is the word **miss?** Fill in the bubble under the word **miss.** (Allow time for the students to fill in their answers.) You should have filled in the first bubble. If you did not, cross out your answer and fill in the first bubble now.

It's time to stop. You did a good job filling in the bubbles. Let's go over your answers. **(Review the answers with the children. Collect the test pages.)**

Lesson 37

Name ______________________ Date ______________

1. a ◯ e ◯ i ◯

2.  ◯ ◯  ◯

3. ma ◯ ma ◯ am ◯

4. miss ◯ ram ◯ dare ◯

Lesson 38

(Duplicate the test page for each child and fill in the name and date on each test. Be sure each child has a pencil. Distribute the tests.)

1. Put your finger on row 1. Look at the letters. Which letter makes the first sound you hear in the word **eat?** Fill in the bubble under the letter that makes the first sound in the word **eat.** (Allow time for the students to fill in their answers.) You should have filled in the third bubble. If you did not, cross out your answer and fill in the third bubble now.

2. Touch row 2. Look at the answers. Which answer makes the sound **thththh?** Fill in the bubble under the answer that makes the sound **thththh.** (Allow time for the students to fill in their answers.) You should have filled in the third bubble. If you did not, cross out your answer and fill in the third bubble now.

3. Touch row 3. Look at the pictures. They show a seed, a mat, and a leaf. Which picture has a different middle sound from the others? Fill in the bubble under the picture that has a different middle sound. (Allow time for the students to fill in their answers.) You should have filled in the second bubble. If you did not, cross out your answer and fill in the second bubble now.

4. Touch row 4. Look at the answers. Which answer is the word **if?** Fill in the bubble under the word **if.** (Allow time for the students to fill in their answers.) You should have filled in the first bubble. If you did not, cross out your answer and fill in the first bubble now.

It's time to stop. You did a good job filling in the bubbles. Let's go over your answers. **(Review the answers with the children. Collect the test pages.)**

Lesson 38

Name ______________________ Date ______________

1. i ◯ a ◯ e ◯

2. dr ◯ fr ◯ th ◯

3.  ◯ 

◯  ◯

4. if ◯ is ◯ as ◯

Lesson 39

(Duplicate the test page for each child and fill in the name and date on each test. Be sure each child has a pencil. Distribute the tests.)

1. Put your finger on row 1. Look at the letters. Which letters make the last sound you hear in the word **bath?** Fill in the bubble under the answer that makes the last sound in the word **bath.** (Allow time for the students to fill in their answers.) You should have filled in the first bubble. If you did not, cross out your answer and fill in the first bubble now.

2. Touch row 2. Look at the pictures. Which picture helps people put out a fire? Fill in the bubble under the picture of something that helps people put out a fire. (Allow time for the students to fill in their answers.) You should have filled in the second bubble. If you did not, cross out your answer and fill in the second bubble now.

3. Touch row 3. Look at the pictures. Which picture shows a **bee?** Fill in the bubble under the picture of the **bee.** (Allow time for the students to fill in their answers.) You should have filled in the second bubble. If you did not, cross out your answer and fill in the second bubble now.

4. Touch row 4. Look at the answers. Which answer is the word **sad?** Fill in the bubble under the word **sad.** (Allow time for the students to fill in their answers.) You should have filled in the third bubble. If you did not, cross out your answer and fill in the third bubble now.

It's time to stop. You did a good job filling in the bubbles. Let's go over your answers. **(Review the answers with the children. Collect the test pages.)**

Lesson 39

Name ______________________ Date ____________

1. th ◯ rd ◯ ms ◯

2. 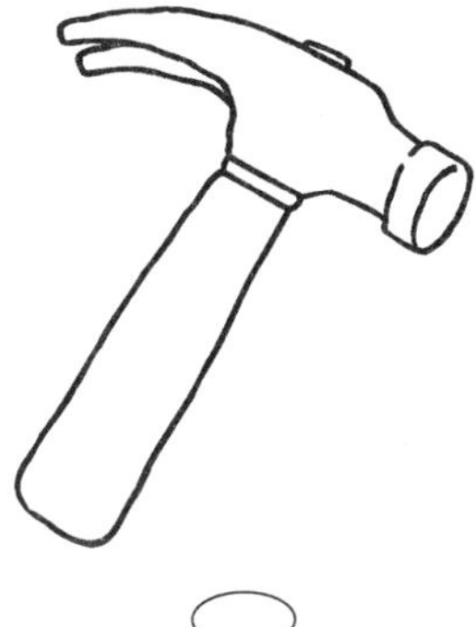 ◯ 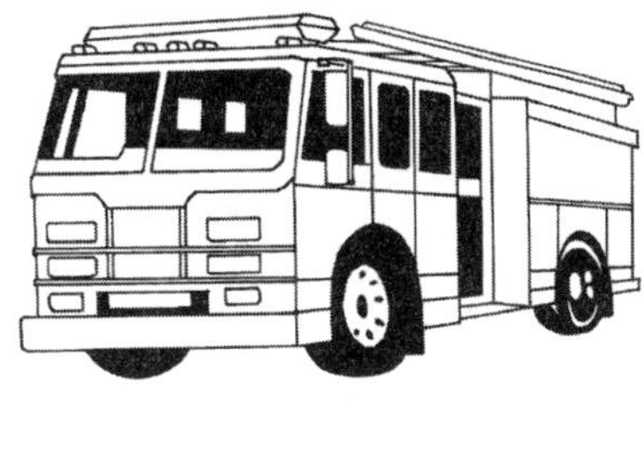 ◯ 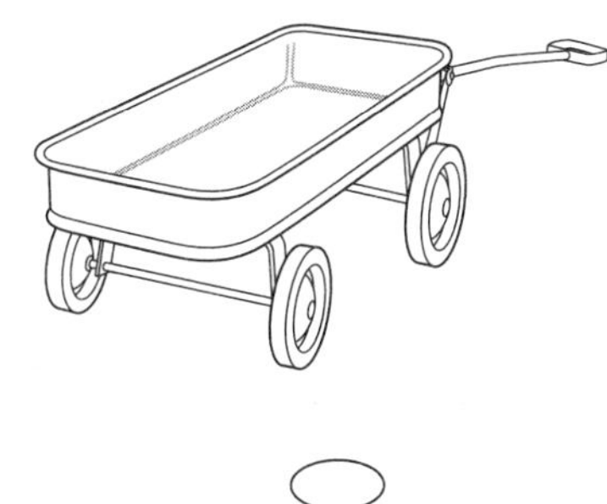 ◯

3.  ◯  ◯  ◯

4. 

◯ dim ◯ sad ◯

Lesson 40

(Duplicate the test page for each child and fill in the name and date on each test. Be sure each child has a pencil. Distribute the tests.)

Today we are going to do something different. I am going to read a story out loud. Then we will answer some questions about the story. Listen carefully. (Read the story out loud.)

The Zoo Trip

The children visited the zoo. They rode to the zoo in a bus.
The lion was the animal the children liked best. It was taking a nap. Then it woke up.
The lion yawned and showed his teeth.

Now we will answer the questions.

1 Put your finger on row 1. Look at the pictures. They show a monkey, a lion, and a seal. Which picture shows the animal the children liked best? Fill in the bubble under the animal the children liked best. (Allow time for the students to fill in their answers.) You should have filled in the second bubble. If you did not, cross out your answer and fill in the second bubble now.

2 Touch row 2. Look at the pictures. They show a bus, a car, and a train. Which picture shows how the students got to the zoo? Fill in the bubble under the picture that shows how the students got to the zoo. (Allow time for the students to fill in their answers.) You should have filled in the first bubble. If you did not, cross out your answer and fill in the first bubble now.

It's time to stop. You did a good job filling in the bubbles. Let's go over your answers. **(Review the answers with the children. Collect the test pages.)**

Lesson 40

Name ______________________ Date ______________

1

2

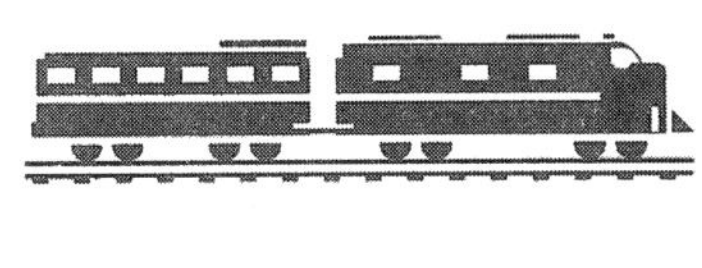

Lesson 41

(Duplicate the test page for each child and fill in the name and date on each test. Be sure each child has a pencil. Distribute the tests.)

1. Put your finger on row 1. Look at the pictures. Which picture shows money? Fill in the bubble under the money. **(Allow time for the students to fill in their answers.)** You should have filled in the second bubble. If you did not, cross out your answer and fill in the second bubble now.

2. Touch row 2. Look at the letters. Which letter makes the sound **t?** Fill in the bubble under the letter that makes the sound **t.** **(Allow time for the students to fill in their answers.)** You should have filled in the first bubble. If you did not, cross out your answer and fill in the first bubble now.

3. Touch row 3. Look at the pictures. They show a desk, a ring, and a sock. Which answer begins with the same sound as **do?** Fill in the bubble under the answer that begins with the same sound as **do.** **(Allow time for the students to fill in their answers.)** You should have filled in the first bubble. If you did not, cross out your answer and fill in the first bubble now.

4. Touch row 4. Look at the answers. Which answer is the word **add?** Fill in the bubble under the word **add.** **(Allow time for the students to fill in their answers.)** You should have filled in the third bubble. If you did not, cross out your answer and fill in the third bubble now.

It's time to stop. You did a good job filling in the bubbles. Let's go over your answers. **(Review the answers with the children. Collect the test pages.)**

Lesson 41

Name ______________________ Date ______________

1

2 t m r

3

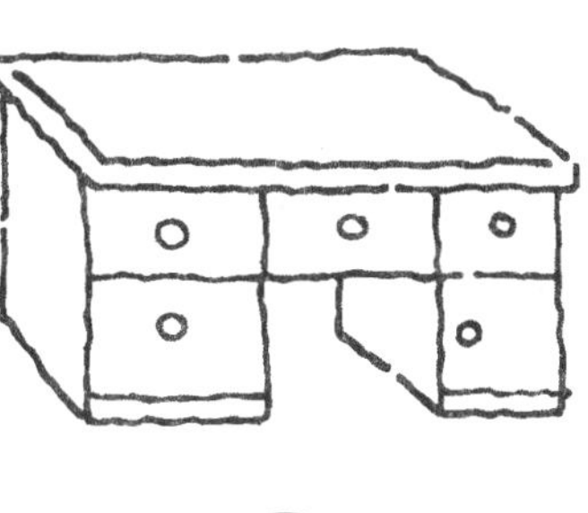

4 ear dim add

Lesson 42

(Duplicate the test page for each child and fill in the name and date on each test. Be sure each child has a pencil. Distribute the tests.)

1. Put your finger on row 1. Look at the pictures. They show a net, a bus, and a frog. Which one ends with the sound **t?** Fill in the bubble under the picture that ends with the sound **t.** (Allow time for the students to fill in their answers.) You should have filled in the first bubble. If you did not, cross out your answer and fill in the first bubble now.

2. Touch row 2. Look at the answers. Two of the answers are the same, and one is different. Which answer is different? Fill in the bubble under the answer that is different. (Allow time for the students to fill in their answers.) You should have filled in the third bubble. If you did not, cross out your answer and fill in the third bubble now.

3. Touch row 3. Look at the pictures. They show a boot, a weed, and a belt. Which picture rhymes with **seed?** Fill in the bubble under the picture that rhymes with **seed.** (Allow time for the students to fill in their answers.) You should have filled in the second bubble. If you did not, cross out your answer and fill in the second bubble now.

4. Touch row 4. Look at the answers. Which answer is the word **the?** Fill in the bubble under the word **the.** (Allow time for the students to fill in their answers.) You should have filled in the first bubble. If you did not, cross out your answer and fill in the first bubble now.

It's time to stop. You did a good job filling in the bubbles. Let's go over your answers. **(Review the answers with the children. Collect the test pages.)**

Lesson
42

Name ______________________________ Date ________________

1

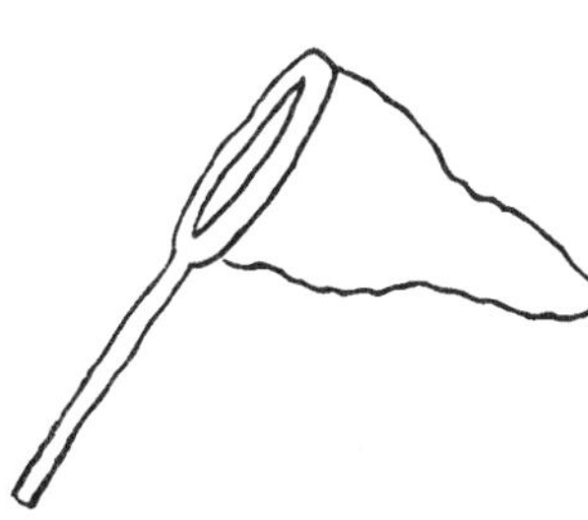

2

f

3

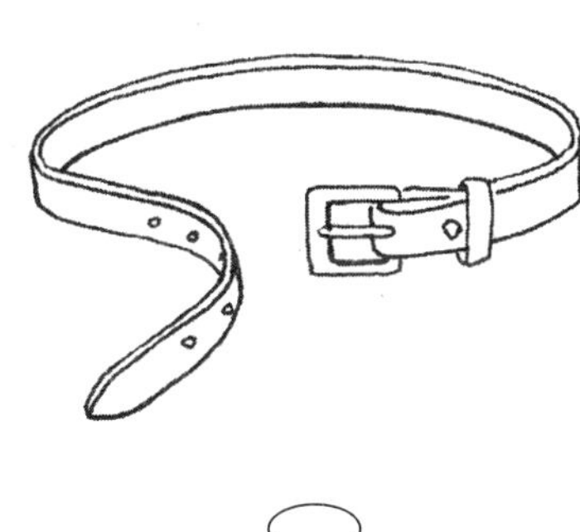

4

is

me

Lesson 43

(Duplicate the test page for each child and fill in the name and date on each test. Be sure each child has a pencil. Distribute the tests.)

1. Put your finger on row 1. Look at the pictures. Which picture shows a **tiger?** Fill in the bubble under the picture of the **tiger.** (Allow time for the students to fill in their answers.) You should have filled in the first bubble. If you did not, cross out your answer and fill in the first bubble now.

2. Touch row 2. Look at the answers. Which answer makes the sound you hear at the beginning of the word **top?** Fill in the bubble under the answer that makes the beginning sound in the word **top.** (Allow time for the students to fill in their answers.) You should have filled in the second bubble. If you did not, cross out your answer and fill in the second bubble now.

3. Touch row 3. Look at the pictures. They show a nose, a foot, and a hand. Which answer has the same middle sound as **lamp?** Fill in the bubble under the answer that has the same middle sound as **lamp.** (Allow time for the students to fill in their answers.) You should have filled in the third bubble. If you did not, cross out your answer and fill in the third bubble now.

4. Touch row 4. Look at the answers. Which answer is the word **is?** Fill in the bubble under the word **is.** (Allow time for the students to fill in their answers.) You should have filled in the first bubble. If you did not, cross out your answer and fill in the first bubble now.

It's time to stop. You did a good job filling in the bubbles. Let's go over your answers. **(Review the answers with the children. Collect the test pages.)**

Lesson 43

Name ______________________ Date ______________

1

2

m

t

f

3

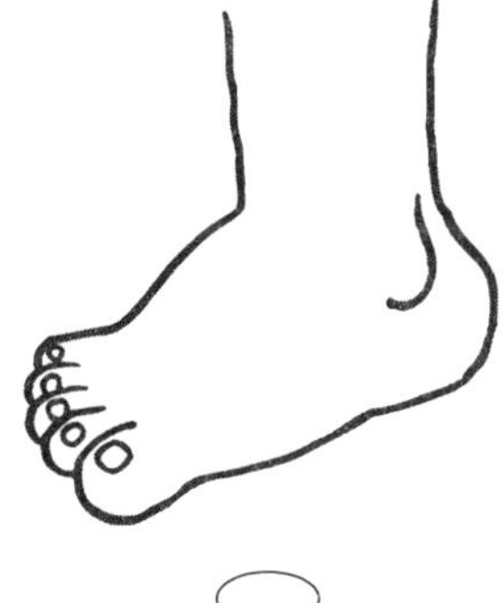

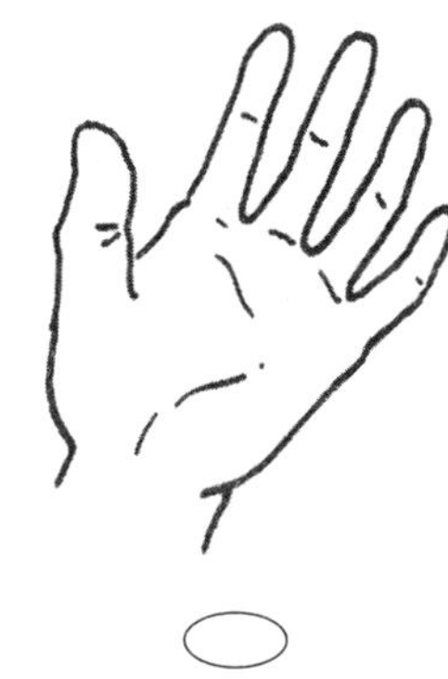

4

is

am

if

Lesson 44

(Duplicate the test page for each child and fill in the name and date on each test. Be sure each child has a pencil. Distribute the tests.)

1 Put your finger on row 1. Look at the pictures. Which picture shows a **monkey?** Fill in the bubble under the picture of the **monkey.** (Allow time for the students to fill in their answers.) You should have filled in the second bubble. If you did not, cross out your answer and fill in the second bubble now.

2 Touch row 2. Look at the letters. Which letter makes the sound **nnn?** Fill in the bubble under the letter that makes the sound **nnn.** (Allow time for the students to fill in their answers.) You should have filled in the third bubble. If you did not, cross out your answer and fill in the third bubble now.

3 Touch row 3. Look at the pictures. They show a moth, a horse, and a mouse. Which answer ends with the same sound as **with?** Fill in the bubble under the answer that ends with the same sound as **with.** (Allow time for the students to fill in their answers.) You should have filled in the first bubble. If you did not, cross out your answer and fill in the first bubble now.

4 Touch row 4. Look at the answers. Which answer is the word **that?** Fill in the bubble under the word **that.** (Allow time for the students to fill in their answers.) You should have filled in the second bubble. If you did not, cross out your answer and fill in the second bubble now.

It's time to stop. You did a good job filling in the bubbles. Let's go over your answers. **(Review the answers with the children. Collect the test pages.)**

Lesson 44

Name ______________________ Date ______________

1

2

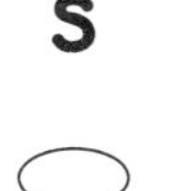

s

r

n

3

4

mad

that

fan

(Duplicate the test page for each child and fill in the name and date on each test. Be sure each child has a pencil. Distribute the tests.)

1 Put your finger on row 1. Look at the pictures. Which picture shows *a boy with a sack?* Fill in the bubble under the picture of *a boy with a sack.* (Allow time for the students to fill in their answers.) You should have filled in the third bubble. If you did not, cross out your answer and fill in the third bubble now.

2 Touch row 2. Look at the answers. Which answer shows **iii nnn?** Fill in the bubble under the answer that shows **iii nnn.** (Allow time for the students to fill in their answers.) You should have filled in the third bubble. If you did not, cross out your answer and fill in the third bubble now.

3 Touch row 3. Look at the pictures. They show a knife, a fork, and a spoon. Which picture begins with the same sound as **note?** Fill in the bubble under the answer that begins with the same sound as **note.** (Allow time for the students to fill in their answers.) You should have filled in the first bubble. If you did not, cross out your answer and fill in the first bubble now.

4 Touch row 4. Look at the answers. Which answer is the word **tear?** Fill in the bubble under the word **tear.** (Note to teacher: *tear* is pronounced *teer.*) (Allow time for the students to fill in their answers.) You should have filled in the second bubble. If you did not, cross out your answer and fill in the second bubble now.

It's time to stop. You did a good job filling in the bubbles. Let's go over your answers. **(Review the answers with the children. Collect the test pages.)**

Lesson 45

Name ______________________ Date ______________

1

2

an if in

3

4

seem tear that

(Duplicate the test page for each child and fill in the name and date on each test. Be sure each child has a pencil. Distribute the tests.)

1 Put your finger on row 1. Look at the pictures. Which picture shows something you might make when it snows? Fill in the bubble under the picture that shows something you might make when it snows. (Allow time for the students to fill in their answers.) You should have filled in the second bubble. If you did not, cross out your answer and fill in the second bubble now.

2 Touch row 2. Look at the letters. Which letter makes the first sound you hear in the word **no?** Fill in the bubble under the letter that makes the first sound in the word **no.** (Allow time for the students to fill in their answers.) You should have filled in the third bubble. If you did not, cross out your answer and fill in the third bubble now.

3 Touch row 3. Look at the pictures. They show a clam, a crab, and a gull. Which picture rhymes with **am?** Fill in the bubble under the picture that rhymes with **am.** (Allow time for the students to fill in their answers.) You should have filled in the first bubble. If you did not, cross out your answer and fill in the first bubble now.

4 Touch row 4. Look at the answers. Which answer is the word **meat?** Fill in the bubble under the word **meat.** (Allow time for the students to fill in their answers.) You should have filled in the first bubble. If you did not, cross out your answer and fill in the first bubble now.

It's time to stop. You did a good job filling in the bubbles. Let's go over your answers. **(Review the answers with the children. Collect the test pages.)**

Lesson 46

Name ______________________ Date ______________

❶

❷ s r n

❸

❹ meat team near

(Duplicate the test page for each child and fill in the name and date on each test. Be sure each child has a pencil. Distribute the tests.)

1 Put your finger on row 1. Look at the pictures. Which animal has a fin? Fill in the bubble under the animal that has a fin. (Allow time for the students to fill in their answers.) You should have filled in the first bubble. If you did not, cross out your answer and fill in the first bubble now.

2 Touch row 2. Look at the letters. Which letter makes the sound you hear at the end of the word **team?** Fill in the bubble under the letter that makes the sound you hear at the end of the word **team.** (Allow time for the students to fill in their answers.) You should have filled in the second bubble. If you did not, cross out your answer and fill in the second bubble now.

3 Touch row 3. Look at the words. Two of the words are the same and one is different. Which word is different? Fill in the bubble under the word that is different. (Allow time for the students to fill in their answers.) You should have filled in the second bubble. If you did not, cross out your answer and fill in the second bubble now.

4 Touch row 4. Look at the answers. Which answer is the word **tin?** Fill in the bubble under the word **tin.** (Allow time for the students to fill in their answers.) You should have filled in the third bubble. If you did not, cross out your answer and fill in the third bubble now.

It's time to stop. You did a good job filling in the bubbles. Let's go over your answers. **(Review the answers with the children. Collect the test pages.)**

Name ______________________ Date ______________

1

  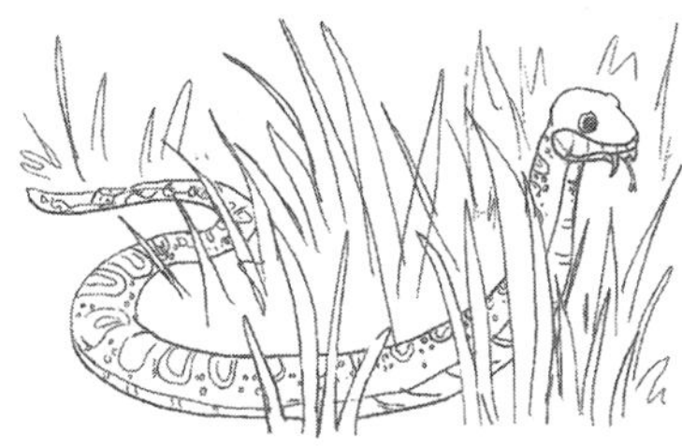

2 t m e

3 sit fit sit

4 sat net tin

Lesson 48

(Duplicate the test page for each child and fill in the name and date on each test. Be sure each child has a pencil. Distribute the tests.)

1. Put your finger on row 1. Look at the pictures. They show a rug, a van, and a tent. Which answer begins with the sound **vvv?** Fill in the bubble under the answer that begins with the sound **vvv.** (Allow time for the students to fill in their answers.) You should have filled in the second bubble. If you did not, cross out your answer and fill in the second bubble now.

2. Touch row 2. Look at the letters. Which letter makes the sound **c?** Fill in the bubble under the letter that makes the sound **c.** (Note to teacher: *c* is pronounced **k.**) (Allow time for the students to fill in their answers.) You should have filled in the first bubble. If you did not, cross out your answer and fill in the first bubble now.

3. Touch row 3. Look at the pictures. Which picture goes with the words *rides a horse?* Fill in the bubble under the picture that goes with the words *rides a horse.* (Allow time for the students to fill in their answers.) You should have filled in the third bubble. If you did not, cross out your answer and fill in the third bubble now.

4. Touch row 4. Look at the answers. Which answer is the word **ran?** Fill in the bubble under the word **ran.** (Allow time for the students to fill in their answers.) You should have filled in the third bubble. If you did not, cross out your answer and fill in the third bubble now.

It's time to stop. You did a good job filling in the bubbles. Let's go over your answers. **(Review the answers with the children. Collect the test pages.)**

Lesson 48

Name ____________________ Date ____________

1

2

c

r

m

3

4

tan

fan

ran

(Duplicate the test page for each child and fill in the name and date on each test. Be sure each child has a pencil. Distribute the tests.)

1 Put your finger on row 1. Look at the pictures. They show a car, a bird, and a log. Which answer has the same beginning sound as **can?** Fill in the bubble under the answer that has the same beginning sound as **can.** (Allow time for the students to fill in their answers.) You should have filled in the first bubble. If you did not, cross out your answer and fill in the first bubble now.

2 Touch row 2. Look at the words. Which words ends with the sound **ththth?** Fill in the bubble under the word that ends with the sound **ththth.** (Allow time for the students to fill in their answers.) You should have filled in the third bubble. If you did not, cross out your answer and fill in the third bubble now.

3 Touch row 3. Look at the pictures. Which picture goes with the words *something you can eat?* Fill in the bubble under the picture that goes with the words *something you can eat.* (Allow time for the students to fill in their answers.) You should have filled in the second bubble. If you did not, cross out your answer and fill in the second bubble now.

4 Touch row 4. Look at the answers. Which answer is the word **mean?** Fill in the bubble under the word **mean.** (Allow time for the students to fill in their answers.) You should have filled in the third bubble. If you did not, cross out your answer and fill in the third bubble now.

It's time to stop. You did a good job filling in the bubbles. Let's go over your answers. **(Review the answers with the children. Collect the test pages.)**

Lesson 49

Name ____________________ Date ____________

1

2 most dear both

3

4 seem team mean

(Duplicate the test page for each child and fill in the name and date on each test. Be sure each child has a pencil. Distribute the tests.)

1. Put your finger on row 1. Look at the pictures. Which picture begins with the sound **c?** Fill in the bubble under the picture that begins with the sound **c.** (Allow time for the students to fill in their answers.) You should have filled in the third bubble. If you did not, cross out your answer and fill in the third bubble now.

2. Touch row 2. Look at the words. Which word begins with the sound **fff?** Fill in the bubble under the answer that begins with the sound **fff.** (Allow time for the students to fill in their answers.) You should have filled in the first bubble. If you did not, cross out your answer and fill in the first bubble now.

3. Touch row 3. Look at the pictures. Which picture goes with the words *a place where a dog lives?* Fill in the bubble under the picture that goes with the words *a place where a dog lives.* (Allow time for the students to fill in their answers.) You should have filled in the first bubble. If you did not, cross out your answer and fill in the first bubble now.

4. Touch row 4. Look at the answers. Which answer is the word **this?** Fill in the bubble under the word **this.** (Allow time for the students to fill in their answers.) You should have filled in the second bubble. If you did not, cross out your answer and fill in the second bubble now.

It's time to stop. You did a good job filling in the bubbles. Let's go over your answers. **(Review the answers with the children. Collect the test pages.)**

Lesson 50

Name ______________________ Date ______________

1

2

fat

mat

rat

3

4

then

this

than

Lesson 51

(Duplicate the test page for each child and fill in the name and date on each test. Be sure each child has a pencil. Distribute the tests.)

1. Put your finger on row 1. Look at the letters. Which letter makes the sound **ooo?** Fill in the bubble under the letter that makes the sound **ooo.** (Note to teacher: This is the short o sound as in *rock*.) (Allow time for the students to fill in their answers.) You should have filled in the third bubble. If you did not, cross out your answer and fill in the third bubble now.

2. Touch row 2. Look at the pictures. Which picture goes with the words *keeps you cool?* Fill in the bubble under the picture that goes with the words *keeps you cool.* (Allow time for the students to fill in their answers.) You should have filled in the second bubble. If you did not, cross out your answer and fill in the second bubble now.

3. Touch row 3. Look at the answers. Which answer means **went fast?** Fill in the bubble under the word that means **went fast.** (Allow time for the students to fill in their answers.) You should have filled in the third bubble. If you did not, cross out your answer and fill in the third bubble now.

4. Touch row 4. Look at the answers. Which answer is the word **can?** Fill in the bubble under the word **can.** (Allow time for the students to fill in their answers.) You should have filled in the first bubble. If you did not, cross out your answer and fill in the first bubble now.

It's time to stop. You did a good job filling in the bubbles. Let's go over your answers. **(Review the answers with the children. Collect the test pages.)**

Name ______________________ Date ______________

1 e ○ i ○ o ○

2

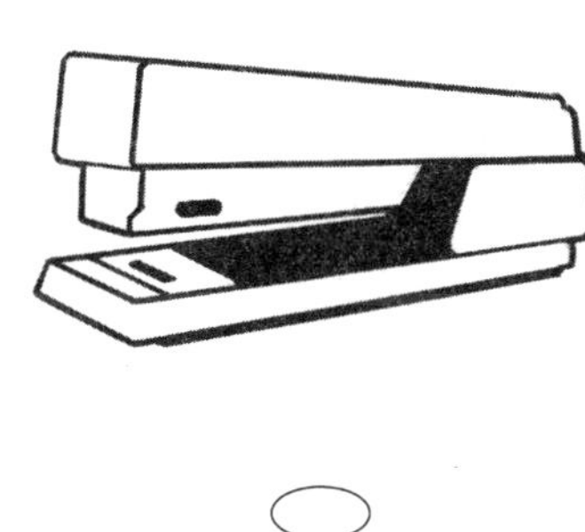

○ ○ ○

3 sat ○ and ○ ran ○

4 can ○ man ○ car ○

(Duplicate the test page for each child and fill in the name and date on each test. Be sure each child has a pencil. Distribute the tests.)

1 Put your finger on row 1. Look at the pictures. They show a box, a coat, and a sack. Which answer has the same middle sound as **hot?** Fill in the bubble under the answer that has the same middle sound as **hot.** (Allow time for the students to fill in their answers.) You should have filled in the first bubble. If you did not, cross out your answer and fill in the first bubble now.

2 Touch row 2. Look at the words. Two of the words are the same and one is different. Which word is different? Fill in the bubble under the word that is different. (Allow time for the students to fill in their answers.) You should have filled in the second bubble. If you did not, cross out your answer and fill in the second bubble now.

3 Touch row 3. Look at the pictures. Which picture goes with the words *sitting by a stream?* Fill in the bubble under the picture that goes with the words *sitting by a stream.* (Allow time for the students to fill in their answers.) You should have filled in the third bubble. If you did not, cross out your answer and fill in the third bubble now.

4 Touch row 4. Look at the answers. Which answer is the word **not?** Fill in the bubble under the word **not.** (Allow time for the students to fill in their answers.) You should have filled in the third bubble. If you did not, cross out your answer and fill in the third bubble now.

It's time to stop. You did a good job filling in the bubbles. Let's go over your answers. **(Review the answers with the children. Collect the test pages.)**

Lesson 52

Name ______________________ Date ______________

❶

❷ an on an

❸

❹ the sad not

Lesson 53

(Duplicate the test page for each child and fill in the name and date on each test. Be sure each child has a pencil. Distribute the tests.)

1. Put your finger on row 1. Look at the pictures. Which picture shows a **wagon?** Fill in the bubble under the picture of the **wagon.** (Allow time for the students to fill in their answers.) You should have filled in the second bubble. If you did not, cross out your answer and fill in the second bubble now.

2. Touch row 2. Look at the answers. Which answer rhymes with **mad?** Fill in the bubble under the word that rhymes with **mad.** (Allow time for the students to fill in their answers.) You should have filled in the first bubble. If you did not, cross out your answer and fill in the first bubble now.

3. Touch row 3. Which answer makes the sound you hear at the beginning of the word **ox?** Fill in the bubble under the answer that makes the beginning sound in the word **ox.** (Allow time for the students to fill in their answers.) You should have filled in the second bubble. If you did not, cross out your answer and fill in the second bubble now.

4. Touch row 4. Look at the answers. Which answer is the word **neat?** Fill in the bubble under the word **neat.** (Allow time for the students to fill in their answers.) You should have filled in the third bubble. If you did not, cross out your answer and fill in the third bubble now.

It's time to stop. You did a good job filling in the bubbles. Let's go over your answers. **(Review the answers with the children. Collect the test pages.)**

Lesson 53

Name ______________________ Date ______________

1

2 sad fan car

3 e o i

4 team feed neat

Lesson 54

(Duplicate the test page for each child and fill in the name and date on each test. Be sure each child has a pencil. Distribute the tests.)

1. Put your finger on row 1. Look at the words. (Note to teacher: *c* is pronounced **k.**) Which word begins with the sound **c?** Fill in the bubble under the word that begins with the sound **c.** (Allow time for the students to fill in their answers.) You should have filled in the second bubble. If you did not, cross out your answer and fill in the second bubble now.

2. Touch row 2. Look at the pictures. Which picture is something that might make people mad? Fill in the bubble under the picture of something that might make people mad. (Allow time for the students to fill in their answers.) You should have filled in the second bubble. If you did not, cross out your answer and fill in the second bubble now.

3. Touch row 3. Look at the words. Two of the words are the same and one is different. Which word is different? Fill in the bubble under the word that is different. (Allow time for the students to fill in their answers.) You should have filled in the third bubble. If you did not, cross out your answer and fill in the third bubble now.

4. Touch row 4. Look at the answers. Which answer is the word **tin?** Fill in the bubble under the word **tin.** (Allow time for the students to fill in their answers.) You should have filled in the first bubble. If you did not, cross out your answer and fill in the first bubble now.

It's time to stop. You did a good job filling in the bubbles. Let's go over your answers. **(Review the answers with the children. Collect the test pages.)**

Lesson 54

Name ______________________ Date ______________

1 rim ○ cat ○ fit ○

2  ○ ○  ○

3 ton ○ ton ○ not ○

4 tin ○ not ○ ran ○

(Duplicate the test page for each child and fill in the name and date on each test. Be sure each child has a pencil. Distribute the tests.)

1 Put your finger on row 1. Look at the pictures. Which answer shows a fat cat? Fill in the bubble under the answer that shows a fat cat. (Allow time for the students to fill in their answers.) You should have filled in the third bubble. If you did not, cross out your answer and fill in the third bubble now.

2 Touch row 2. Look at the answers. Which answer means a kind of animal? Fill in the bubble under the word that means a kind of animal. (Allow time for the students to fill in their answers.) You should have filled in the first bubble. If you did not, cross out your answer and fill in the first bubble now.

3 Touch row 3. Look at the pictures. They show a pot, a tack, and a deer. Which picture rhymes with **ack?** Fill in the bubble under the picture that rhymes with **ack.** (Allow time for the students to fill in their answers.) You should have filled in the second bubble. If you did not, cross out your answer and fill in the second bubble now.

4 Touch row 4. Look at the answers. Which answer is the word **tack?** Fill in the bubble under the word **tack.** (Allow time for the students to fill in their answers.) You should have filled in the third bubble. If you did not, cross out your answer and fill in the third bubble now.

It's time to stop. You did a good job filling in the bubbles. Let's go over your answers. **(Review the answers with the children. Collect the test pages.)**

Lesson 55

Name ______________________ Date ______________

❶

❷ rat mat sat

❸

❹ rock sick tack

Lesson 56

(Duplicate the test page for each child and fill in the name and date on each test. Be sure each child has a pencil. Distribute the tests.)

1. Put your finger on row 1. Look at the pictures. Which picture goes with the words *not a dog?* Fill in the bubble under the picture that goes with the words *not a dog.* **(Allow time for the students to fill in their answers.)** You should have filled in the first bubble. If you did not, cross out your answer and fill in the first bubble now.

2. Touch row 2. Look at the letters. Which letter makes the middle sound you hear in the word **meet?** Fill in the bubble under the letter that makes the middle sound in the word **meet. (Allow time for the students to fill in their answers.)** You should have filled in the third bubble. If you did not, cross out your answer and fill in the third bubble now.

3. Touch row 3. Look at the answers. Which answer shows **fff rrr?** Fill in the bubble under the answer that shows **fff rrr. (Allow time for the students to fill in their answers.)** You should have filled in the first bubble. If you did not, cross out your answer and fill in the first bubble now.

4. Touch row 4. Look at the answers. Which answer is the word **sick?** Fill in the bubble under the word **sick. (Allow time for the students to fill in their answers.)** You should have filled in the second bubble. If you did not, cross out your answer and fill in the second bubble now.

It's time to stop. You did a good job filling in the bubbles. Let's go over your answers.
(Review the answers with the children. Collect the test pages.)

Lesson 56

Name ______________________ Date ______________

1  ◯ ◯  ◯

2 a ◯ i ◯ e ◯

3 fr ◯ if ◯ tr ◯

4 thin ◯ sick ◯ rock ◯

Lesson 57

(Duplicate the test page for each child and fill in the name and date on each test. Be sure each child has a pencil. Distribute the tests.)

1. Put your finger on row 1. Look at the pictures. Which picture shows a **light bulb?** Fill in the bubble under the picture of the **light bulb.** (Allow time for the students to fill in their answers.) You should have filled in the third bubble. If you did not, cross out your answer and fill in the third bubble now.

2. Touch row 2. Look at the words. Which word rhymes with **meat?** Fill in the bubble under the word that rhymes with **meat.** (Allow time for the students to fill in their answers.) You should have filled in the third bubble. If you did not, cross out your answer and fill in the third bubble now.

3. Touch row 3. Look at the words. Two of the words are the same and one is different. Which word is different? Fill in the bubble under the word that is different. (Allow time for the students to fill in their answers.) You should have filled in the second bubble. If you did not, cross out your answer and fill in the second bubble now.

4. Touch row 4. Look at the answers. Which answer is the word **man?** Fill in the bubble under the word **man.** (Allow time for the students to fill in their answers.) You should have filled in the first bubble. If you did not, cross out your answer and fill in the first bubble now.

It's time to stop. You did a good job filling in the bubbles. Let's go over your answers. **(Review the answers with the children. Collect the test pages.)**

Lesson 57

Name ______________________ Date ______________

1

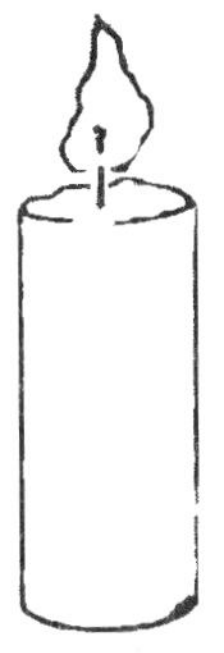

○ ○ ○

2

fish ○ cart ○ seat ○

3

on ○ no ○ on ○

4

man ○ not ○ sad ○

(Duplicate the test page for each child and fill in the name and date on each test. Be sure each child has a pencil. Distribute the tests.)

1 Put your finger on row 1. Look at the pictures. They show a plane, a boat, and a truck. Which answer has the same middle sound as **rain?** Fill in the bubble under the answer that has the same middle sound as **rain.** (Allow time for the students to fill in their answers.) You should have filled in the first bubble. If you did not, cross out your answer and fill in the first bubble now.

2 Touch row 2. Look at the words. Two of the words are the same and one is different. Which word is different? Fill in the bubble under the word that is different. (Allow time for the students to fill in their answers.) You should have filled in the second bubble. If you did not, cross out your answer and fill in the second bubble now.

3 Touch row 3. Look at the answers. Which answer shows **ooo nnn?** Fill in the bubble under the answer that shows **ooo nnn.** (Allow time for the students to fill in their answers.) You should have filled in the third bubble. If you did not, cross out your answer and fill in the third bubble now.

4 Touch row 4. Look at the answers. Which answer is the word **sam?** Fill in the bubble under the word **sam.** (Allow time for the students to fill in their answers.) You should have filled in the first bubble. If you did not, cross out your answer and fill in the first bubble now.

It's time to stop. You did a good job filling in the bubbles. Let's go over your answers.
(Review the answers with the children. Collect the test pages.)

Lesson 58

Name ______________________ Date ______________

1

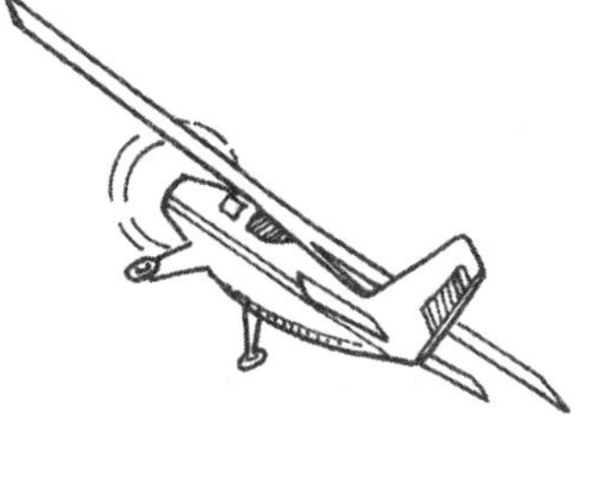

○ ○ ○

2

it ○ sit ○ it ○

3

in ○ no ○ on ○

4

sam ○ mad ○ sat ○

Lesson 59

(Duplicate the test page for each child and fill in the name and date on each test. Be sure each child has a pencil. Distribute the tests.)

1. Put your finger on row 1. Look at the pictures. Which picture shows a **striped shirt?** Fill in the bubble under the picture of the **striped shirt.** (Allow time for the students to fill in their answers.) You should have filled in the second bubble. If you did not, cross out your answer and fill in the second bubble now.

2. Touch row 2. Look at the answers. Which word is **thththaaat?** Fill in the bubble under the word **thththaaat.** (Allow time for the students to fill in their answers.) You should have filled in the first bubble. If you did not, cross out your answer and fill in the first bubble now.

3. Touch row 3. Look at the pictures. Which picture shows a **wheelchair?** Fill in the bubble under the picture of the **wheelchair.** (Allow time for the students to fill in their answers.) You should have filled in the third bubble. If you did not, cross out your answer and fill in the third bubble now.

4. Touch row 4. Look at the answers. Which answer is the word **ate?** Fill in the bubble under the word **ate.** (Allow time for the students to fill in their answers.) You should have filled in the second bubble. If you did not, cross out your answer and fill in the second bubble now.

It's time to stop. You did a good job filling in the bubbles. Let's go over your answers. **(Review the answers with the children. Collect the test pages.)**

Lesson 59

Name ______________________ Date ______________

1

2

that seem rock

3

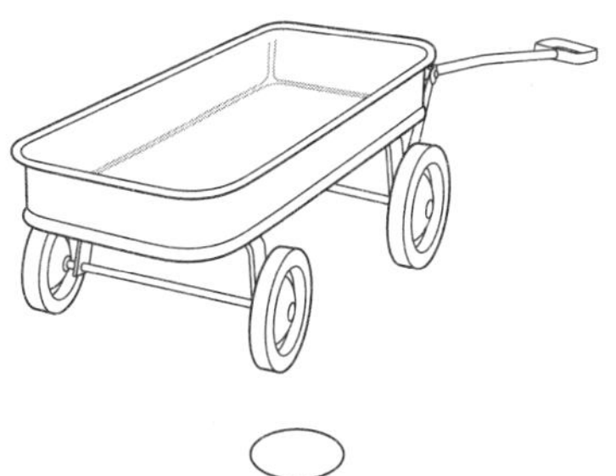

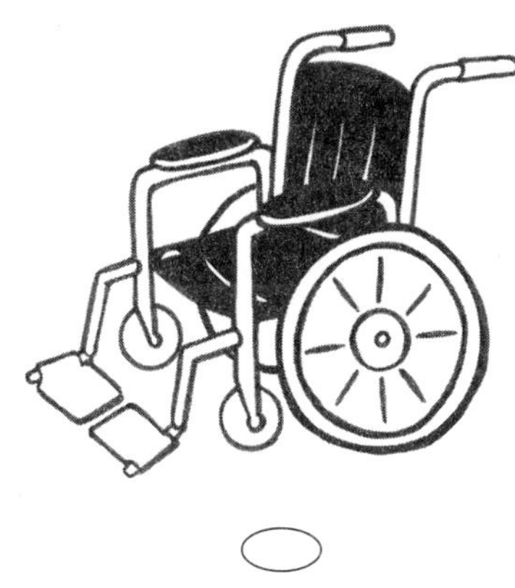

4

not ate sit

(Duplicate the test page for each child and fill in the name and date on each test. Be sure each child has a pencil. Distribute the tests.)

Today we are going to do something different. I am going to read a story out loud. Then we will answer some questions about the story. Listen carefully. (Read the story out loud.)

A Pretty Bird

Jeff heard the bird. It had a pretty song. The bird was on a bush in the swamp.

The bird was almost all black. It had a little spot of color on its wing. Jeff asked Mom what kind of bird it was. She said it was a red-winged blackbird.

Now we will answer the questions.

1. Put your finger on row 1. Look at the pictures. They show a forest, a desert, and a swamp. Which picture shows where Jeff saw the bird? Fill in the bubble under the answer that shows where Jeff saw the bird. (Allow time for the students to fill in their answers.) You should have filled in the third bubble. If you did not, cross out your answer and fill in the third bubble now.

2. Touch row 2. Look at the pictures. Which picture shows the bird that Jeff probably saw? Fill in the bubble under the picture of the bird Jeff probably saw. (Allow time for the students to fill in their answers.) You should have filled in the second bubble. If you did not, cross out your answer and fill in the second bubble now.

It's time to stop. You did a good job filling in the bubbles. Let's go over your answers. **(Review the answers with the children. Collect the test pages.)**

Lesson 60

Name ____________________ Date ____________

1

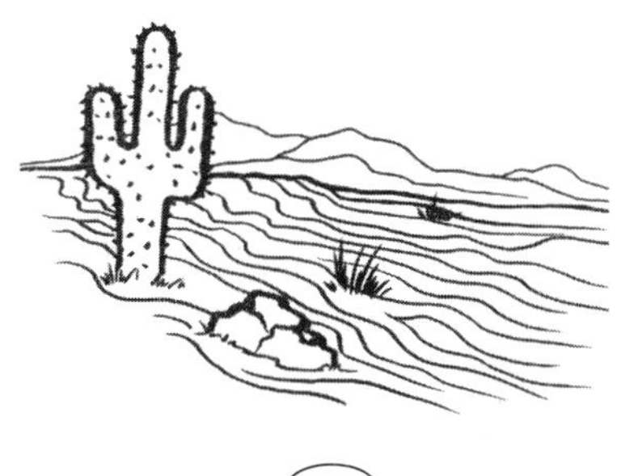

2

Lesson 61

(Duplicate the test page for each child and fill in the name and date on each test. Be sure each child has a pencil. Distribute the tests.)

1. Put your finger on row 1. Look at the letters. Which letter makes the sound **h?** Fill in the bubble under the letter that makes the sound **h.** (Allow time for the students to fill in their answers.) You should have filled in the third bubble. If you did not, cross out your answer and fill in the third bubble now.

2. Touch row 2. Look at the pictures. Which picture shows an **alligator?** Fill in the bubble under the picture of the **alligator.** (Allow time for the students to fill in their answers.) You should have filled in the second bubble. If you did not, cross out your answer and fill in the second bubble now.

3. Touch row 3. Look at the words. Two of the words are the same and one is different. Which word is different? Fill in the bubble under the word that is different. (Allow time for the students to fill in their answers.) You should have filled in the third bubble. If you did not, cross out your answer and fill in the third bubble now.

4. Touch row 4. Look at the answers. Which answer is the word **that?** Fill in the bubble under the word **that.** (Allow time for the students to fill in their answers.) You should have filled in the first bubble. If you did not, cross out your answer and fill in the first bubble now.

It's time to stop. You did a good job filling in the bubbles. **(Collect the test pages.)**

Lesson 61

Name ______________________ Date ______________

1. f ◯ t ◯ h ◯

2.  ◯ ◯  ◯

3. sack ◯ sack ◯ sick ◯

4. that ◯ ate ◯ the ◯

(Duplicate the test page for each child and fill in the name and date on each test. Be sure each child has a pencil. Distribute the tests.)

1. Put your finger on row 1. Look at the pictures. They show a sink, a hose, and a glass. Which answer has the same middle sound as **bit?** Fill in the bubble under the answer that has the same middle sound as **bit.** (Allow time for the students to fill in their answers.) You should have filled in the first bubble. If you did not, cross out your answer and fill in the first bubble now.

2. Touch row 2. Look at the letters. Which letter makes the first sound you hear in the word **house?** Fill in the bubble under the letter that makes the first sound in the word **house.** (Allow time for the students to fill in their answers.) You should have filled in the second bubble. If you did not, cross out your answer and fill in the second bubble now.

3. Touch row 3. Look at the answers. Which answer shows **fff nnn?** Fill in the bubble under the answer that shows **fff nnn.** (Allow time for the students to fill in their answers.) You should have filled in the third bubble. If you did not, cross out your answer and fill in the third bubble now.

4. Touch row 4. Look at the answers. Which answer is the word **rack?** Fill in the bubble under the word **rack.** (Allow time for the students to fill in their answers.) You should have filled in the second bubble. If you did not, cross out your answer and fill in the second bubble now.

It's time to stop. You did a good job filling in the bubbles. **(Collect the test pages.)**

Lesson 62

Name ______________________ Date ______________

❶

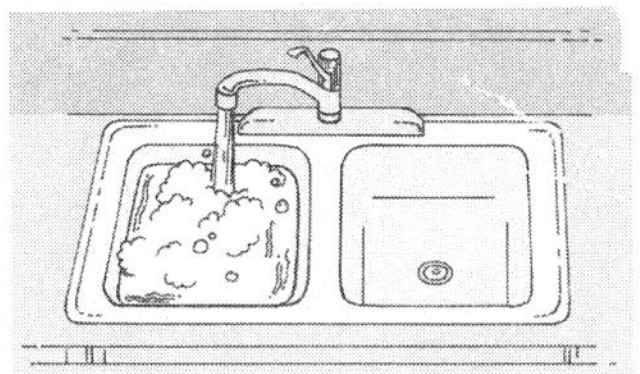

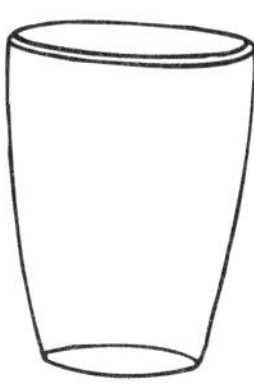

○ ○ ○

❷ m h s

○ ○ ○

❸ dr th fn

○ ○ ○

❹ sick rack sock

○ ○ ○

Lesson 63

(Duplicate the test page for each child and fill in the name and date on each test. Be sure each child has a pencil. Distribute the tests.)

1 Put your finger on row 1. Look at the pictures. Which picture goes with the words *the groceries are in the sack?* Fill in the bubble under the picture that goes with the words *the groceries are in the sack.* **(Allow time for the students to fill in their answers.)** You should have filled in the second bubble. If you did not, cross out your answer and fill in the second bubble now.

2 Touch row 2. Look at the pictures. Which picture goes with the words *something hot?* Fill in the bubble under the picture that goes with the words *something hot.* **(Allow time for the students to fill in their answers.)** You should have filled in the first bubble. If you did not, cross out your answer and fill in the first bubble now.

3 Touch row 3. Look at the words. Which word begins with the sound **h?** Fill in the bubble under the answer that begins with the sound **h.** **(Allow time for the students to fill in their answers.)** You should have filled in the third bubble. If you did not, cross out your answer and fill in the third bubble now.

4 Touch row 4. Look at the answers. Which answer is the word **his?** Fill in the bubble under the word **his.** **(Allow time for the students to fill in their answers.)** You should have filled in the second bubble. If you did not, cross out your answer and fill in the second bubble now.

It's time to stop. You did a good job filling in the bubbles. **(Collect the test pages.)**

Lesson 63

Name ______________________ Date ______________

❶

❷

❸ dot ◯ fat ◯ hit ◯

❹ car ◯ his ◯ mat ◯

(Duplicate the test page for each child and fill in the name and date on each test. Be sure each child has a pencil. Distribute the tests.)

1 Put your finger on row 1. Look at the letters. Which letter makes the first sound you hear in the word **up?** Fill in the bubble under the letter that makes the first sound in the word **up.** (Allow time for the students to fill in their answers.) You should have filled in the third bubble. If you did not, cross out your answer and fill in the third bubble now.

2 Touch row 2. Look at the pictures. Which picture shows a **mitt?** Fill in the bubble under the picture of the **mitt.** (Allow time for the students to fill in their answers.) You should have filled in the second bubble. If you did not, cross out your answer and fill in the second bubble now.

3 Touch row 3. Look at the pictures. Which picture shows a **baseball?** Fill in the bubble under the picture of the **baseball.** (Allow time for the students to fill in their answers.) You should have filled in the third bubble. If you did not, cross out your answer and fill in the third bubble now.

4 Touch row 4. Look at the answers. Which answer is the word **hot?** Fill in the bubble under the word **hot.** (Allow time for the students to fill in their answers.) You should have filled in the first bubble. If you did not, cross out your answer and fill in the first bubble now.

It's time to stop. You did a good job filling in the bubbles. **(Collect the test pages.)**

Lesson 64

Name ______________________ Date ______________

❶ a i u

❷  

❸   

❹ hot sit the

(Duplicate the test page for each child and fill in the name and date on each test. Be sure each child has a pencil. Distribute the tests.)

1. Put your finger on row 1. Look at the pictures. They show a duck, a pig, and a whale. Which answer has the same middle sound as **run?** Fill in the bubble under the answer that has the same middle sound as **run.** (Allow time for the students to fill in their answers.) You should have filled in the first bubble. If you did not, cross out your answer and fill in the first bubble now.

2. Touch row 2. Look at the letters. Two of the letters are the same and one is different. Which letter is different? Fill in the bubble under the letter that is different. (Allow time for the students to fill in their answers.) You should have filled in the second bubble. If you did not, cross out your answer and fill in the second bubble now.

3. Touch row 3. Look at the pictures. Which picture shows a **person?** Fill in the bubble under the picture of the **person.** (Allow time for the students to fill in their answers.) You should have filled in the second bubble. If you did not, cross out your answer and fill in the second bubble now.

4. Touch row 4. Look at the answers. Which answer is the word **not?** Fill in the bubble under the word **not.** (Allow time for the students to fill in their answers.) You should have filled in the third bubble. If you did not, cross out your answer and fill in the third bubble now.

It's time to stop. You did a good job filling in the bubbles. **(Collect the test pages.)**

Lesson 65

Name ____________________ Date ____________

1

2

n u n

3

4

sat had not

(Duplicate the test page for each child and fill in the name and date on each test. Be sure each child has a pencil. Distribute the tests.)

1 Put your finger on row 1. Look at the pictures. Which picture shows a boy sitting on a log? Fill in the bubble under the boy sitting on a log. **(Allow time for the students to fill in their answers.)** You should have filled in the second bubble. If you did not, cross out your answer and fill in the second bubble now.

2 Touch row 2. Look at the answers. Which answer shows **uuu mmm?** Fill in the bubble under the answer that shows **uuu mmm. (Allow time for the students to fill in their answers.)** You should have filled in the first bubble. If you did not, cross out your answer and fill in the first bubble now.

3 Touch row 3. Look at the words. Which word rhymes with **see?** Fill in the bubble under the word that rhymes with **see. (Allow time for the students to fill in their answers.)** You should have filled in the third bubble. If you did not, cross out your answer and fill in the third bubble now.

4 Touch row 4. Look at the answers. Which answer is the word **miss?** Fill in the bubble under the word **miss. (Allow time for the students to fill in their answers.)** You should have filled in the first bubble. If you did not, cross out your answer and fill in the first bubble now.

It's time to stop. You did a good job filling in the bubbles. **(Collect the test pages.)**

Name ______________________ Date ____________

1

○ ○ ○

2 um ○ em ○ am ○

3 on ○ it ○ he ○

4 miss ○ not ○ man ○

(Duplicate the test page for each child and fill in the name and date on each test. Be sure each child has a pencil. Distribute the tests.)

1. Put your finger on row 1. Look at the pictures. Which picture goes with the words *he feels sick?* Fill in the bubble under the picture that goes with the words *he feels sick.* **(Allow time for the students to fill in their answers.)** You should have filled in the second bubble. If you did not, cross out your answer and fill in the second bubble now.

2. Touch row 2. Look at the pictures. They show a cup, a jar, and a bowl. Which picture rhymes with **pup?** Fill in the bubble under the picture that rhymes with **pup. (Allow time for the students to fill in their answers.)** You should have filled in the first bubble. If you did not, cross out your answer and fill in the first bubble now.

3. Touch row 3. Look at the words. Which word ends with the sound **nnn?** Fill in the bubble under the word that ends with the sound **nnn. (Allow time for the students to fill in their answers.)** You should have filled in the first bubble. If you did not, cross out your answer and fill in the first bubble now.

4. Touch row 4. Look at the answers. Which answer is the word **nut?** Fill in the bubble under the word **nut. (Allow time for the students to fill in their answers.)** You should have filled in the third bubble. If you did not, cross out your answer and fill in the third bubble now.

It's time to stop. You did a good job filling in the bubbles. **(Collect the test pages.)**

Lesson 67

Name ______________________ Date ______________

1

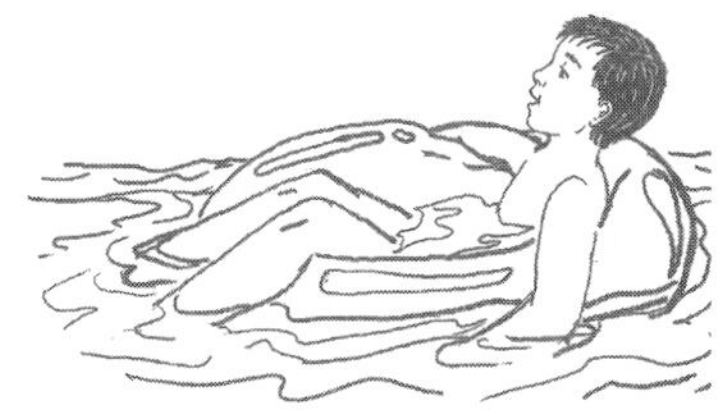

○ ○ ○

2

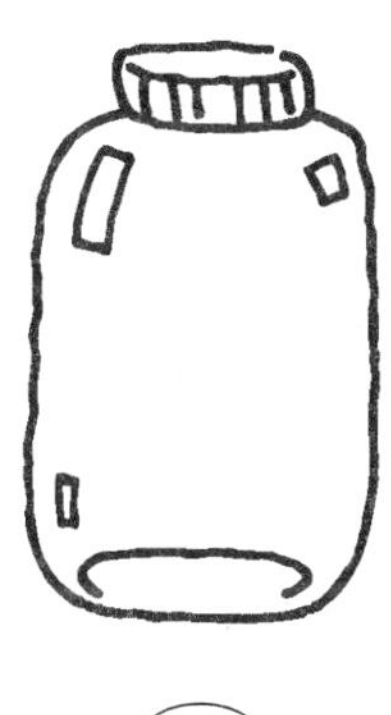

○ ○ ○

3

fun fat far

○ ○ ○

4

not cut nut

○ ○ ○

Lesson 68

(Duplicate the test page for each child and fill in the name and date on each test. Be sure each child has a pencil. Distribute the tests.)

1. Put your finger on row 1. Look at the letters. Which letter makes the sound **g?** Fill in the bubble under the letter that makes the sound **g.** (Allow time for the students to fill in their answers.) You should have filled in the third bubble. If you did not, cross out your answer and fill in the third bubble now.

2. Touch row 2. Look at the pictures. Which picture shows something a dog could really do? Fill in the bubble under the picture of something a dog could really do. (Allow time for the students to fill in their answers.) You should have filled in the first bubble. If you did not, cross out your answer and fill in the first bubble now.

3. Touch row 3. Look at the answers. Which answer shows **fff t?** Fill in the bubble under the answer that shows **fff t.** (Allow time for the students to fill in their answers.) You should have filled in the third bubble. If you did not, cross out your answer and fill in the third bubble now.

4. Touch row 4. Look at the answers. Which answer is the word **has?** Fill in the bubble under the word **has.** (Allow time for the students to fill in their answers.) You should have filled in the first bubble. If you did not, cross out your answer and fill in the first bubble now.

It's time to stop. You did a good job filling in the bubbles. **(Collect the test pages.)**

Lesson 68

Name ______________________ Date ______________

❶ t ◯ f ◯ g ◯

❷

 ◯

 ◯

 ◯

❸ st ◯ fr ◯ ft ◯

❹ has ◯ hat ◯ him ◯

(Duplicate the test page for each child and fill in the name and date on each test. Be sure each child has a pencil. Distribute the tests.)

1. Put your finger on row 1. Look at the pictures. They show a desk, a girl, and a nut. Which answer has the same beginning sound as **get?** Fill in the bubble under the answer that has the same beginning sound as **get.** (Allow time for the students to fill in their answers.) You should have filled in the second bubble. If you did not, cross out your answer and fill in the second bubble now.

2. Touch row 2. Look at the words. Which word has the same beginning sound as **aim?** Fill in the bubble under the answer that has the same beginning sound as **aim.** (Allow time for the students to fill in their answers.) You should have filled in the second bubble. If you did not, cross out your answer and fill in the second bubble now.

3. Touch row 3. Look at the pictures. Which picture shows an **ant?** Fill in the bubble under the picture of the **ant.** (Allow time for the students to fill in their answers.) You should have filled in the first bubble. If you did not, cross out your answer and fill in the first bubble now.

4. Touch row 4. Look at the answers. Which answer is the word **us?** Fill in the bubble under the word **us.** (Allow time for the students to fill in their answers.) You should have filled in the third bubble. If you did not, cross out your answer and fill in the third bubble now.

It's time to stop. You did a good job filling in the bubbles. **(Collect the test pages.)**

Lesson 69

Name ______________________ Date ______________

1

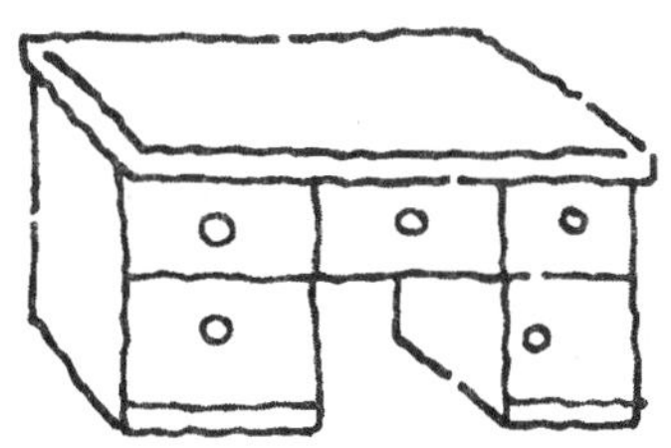

◯ ◯ ◯

2

if ◯

ate ◯

end ◯

3

◯ ◯ ◯

4

up ◯

is ◯

us ◯

Lesson 70

(Duplicate the test page for each child and fill in the name and date on each test. Be sure each child has a pencil. Distribute the tests.)

1. Put your finger on row 1. Look at the pictures. They show a pig, a calf, and a goat. Which one ends with the sound **g?** Fill in the bubble under the picture that ends with the sound **g. (Allow time for the students to fill in their answers.)** You should have filled in the first bubble. If you did not, cross out your answer and fill in the first bubble now.

2. Touch row 2. Look at the words. Which word rhymes with **fade?** Fill in the bubble under the word that rhymes with **fade. (Allow time for the students to fill in their answers.)** You should have filled in the second bubble. If you did not, cross out your answer and fill in the second bubble now.

3. Touch row 3. Look at the pictures. Which picture shows a **hut?** Fill in the bubble under the picture of the **hut. (Allow time for the students to fill in their answers.)** You should have filled in the third bubble. If you did not, cross out your answer and fill in the third bubble now.

4. Touch row 4. Look at the answers. Which answer is the word **rug?** Fill in the bubble under the word **rug. (Allow time for the students to fill in their answers.)** You should have filled in the second bubble. If you did not, cross out your answer and fill in the second bubble now.

It's time to stop. You did a good job filling in the bubbles. **(Collect the test pages.)**

Lesson 70

Name ______________________ Date ______________

1

2

sock

made

mitt

3

4

run

rug

rat

Lesson 71

(Duplicate the test page for each child and fill in the name and date on each test. Be sure each child has a pencil. Distribute the tests.)

1. Put your finger on row 1. Look at the pictures. Which picture goes with the words *makes wind?* Fill in the bubble under the picture that goes with the words *makes wind.* (Allow time for the students to fill in their answers.) You should have filled in the second bubble. If you did not, cross out your answer and fill in the second bubble now.

2. Touch row 2. Look at the words. Which word begins with the same sound as **each?** Fill in the bubble under the answer that begins with the same sound as **each.** (Allow time for the students to fill in their answers.) You should have filled in the third bubble. If you did not, cross out your answer and fill in the third bubble now.

3. Touch row 3. Look at the pictures. Which picture shows something that is hot? Fill in the bubble under the picture of something hot. (Allow time for the students to fill in their answers.) You should have filled in the first bubble. If you did not, cross out your answer and fill in the first bubble now.

4. Touch row 4. Look at the answers. Which answer is the word **dot?** Fill in the bubble under the word **dot.** (Allow time for the students to fill in their answers.) You should have filled in the second bubble. If you did not, cross out your answer and fill in the second bubble now.

It's time to stop. You did a good job filling in the bubbles. **(Collect the test pages.)**

Lesson 71

Name ______________________ Date ______________

1

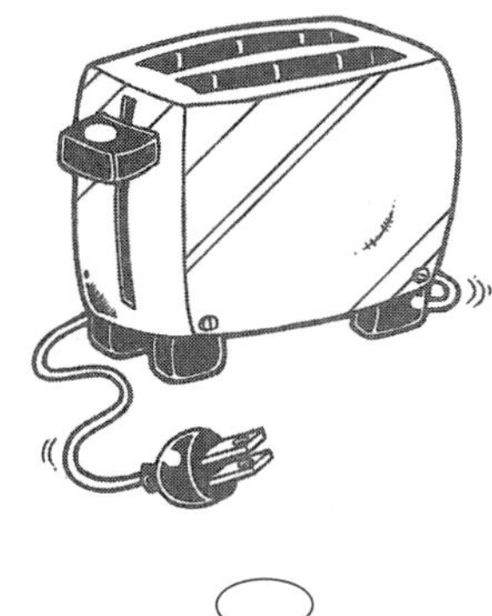

2

odd

and

eat

3

4

rot

dot

not

Lesson 72

(Duplicate the test page for each child and fill in the name and date on each test. Be sure each child has a pencil. Distribute the tests.)

1. Put your finger on row 1. Look at the pictures. Which picture shows a **tiger?** Fill in the bubble under the picture of the **tiger.** (Allow time for the students to fill in their answers.) You should have filled in the third bubble. If you did not, cross out your answer and fill in the third bubble now.

2. Touch row 2. Look at the letters. Which letter makes the sound **lll?** Fill in the bubble under the letter that makes the sound **lll.** (Allow time for the students to fill in their answers.) You should have filled in the second bubble. If you did not, cross out your answer and fill in the second bubble now.

3. Touch row 3. Look at the words. Two of the words are the same and one is different. Which word is different? Fill in the bubble under the word that is different. (Allow time for the students to fill in their answers.) You should have filled in the first bubble. If you did not, cross out your answer and fill in the first bubble now.

4. Touch row 4. Look at the answers. Which answer is the word **has?** Fill in the bubble under the word **has.** (Allow time for the students to fill in their answers.) You should have filled in the third bubble. If you did not, cross out your answer and fill in the third bubble now.

It's time to stop. You did a good job filling in the bubbles. **(Collect the test pages.)**

Lesson 72

Name ______________________ Date ______________

1

○ ○ ○

2

f ○ l ○ t ○

3

he ○ me ○ me ○

4

mad ○ had ○ has ○

(Duplicate the test page for each child and fill in the name and date on each test. Be sure each child has a pencil. Distribute the tests.)

1. Put your finger on row 1. Look at the pictures. They show a lock, a key, and a door. Which answer has the same beginning sound as **let?** Fill in the bubble under the answer that has the same beginning sound as **let.** (Allow time for the students to fill in their answers.) You should have filled in the first bubble. If you did not, cross out your answer and fill in the first bubble now.

2. Touch row 2. Look at the words. Which word has the same middle sound as **wait?** Fill in the bubble under the word that has the same middle sound as **wait.** (Allow time for the students to fill in their answers.) You should have filled in the third bubble. If you did not, cross out your answer and fill in the third bubble now.

3. Touch row 3. Look at the socks. Which sock is biggest? Fill in the bubble under the sock that is biggest. (Allow time for the students to fill in their answers.) You should have filled in the third bubble. If you did not, cross out your answer and fill in the third bubble now.

4. Touch row 4. Look at the answers. Which answer is the word **fig?** Fill in the bubble under the word **fig.** (Allow time for the students to fill in their answers.) You should have filled in the second bubble. If you did not, cross out your answer and fill in the second bubble now.

It's time to stop. You did a good job filling in the bubbles. **(Collect the test pages.)**

Lesson 73

Name ______________________ Date ______________

1

2 feet mean same

3

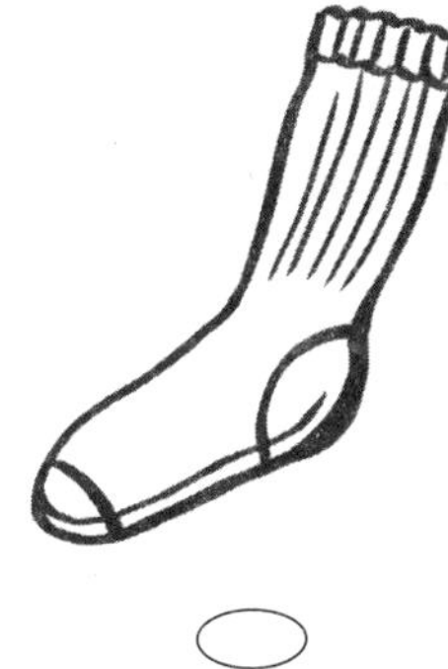

4 fit fig dig

Lesson 74

(Duplicate the test page for each child and fill in the name and date on each test. Be sure each child has a pencil. Distribute the tests.)

1. Put your finger on row 1. Look at the pictures. They show different parts of a plant. Which picture shows a **seed?** Fill in the bubble under the picture of the **seed.** (Allow time for the students to fill in their answers.) You should have filled in the second bubble. If you did not, cross out your answer and fill in the second bubble now.

2. Touch row 2. Look at the answers. Which answer shows **g lll?** Fill in the bubble under the answer that shows **g lll.** (Allow time for the students to fill in their answers.) You should have filled in the third bubble. If you did not, cross out your answer and fill in the third bubble now.

3. Touch row 3. Look at the words. Two of the words are the same and one is different. Which word is different? Fill in the bubble under the word that is different. (Allow time for the students to fill in their answers.) You should have filled in the third bubble. If you did not, cross out your answer and fill in the third bubble now.

4. Touch row 4. Look at the answers. Which answer is the word **mean?** Fill in the bubble under the word **mean.** (Allow time for the students to fill in their answers.) You should have filled in the first bubble. If you did not, cross out your answer and fill in the first bubble now.

It's time to stop. You did a good job filling in the bubbles. **(Collect the test pages.)**

Name ______________________ Date ______________

1

2

ml la gl

3

fate fate late

4

mean meat miss

Lesson 75

(Duplicate the test page for each child and fill in the name and date on each test. Be sure each child has a pencil. Distribute the tests.)

1. Put your finger on row 1. Look at the pictures. Which picture shows a **thermometer?** Fill in the bubble under the picture of the **thermometer.** (Allow time for the students to fill in their answers.) You should have filled in the first bubble. If you did not, cross out your answer and fill in the first bubble now.

2. Touch row 2. Look at the words. Which word begins with the sound **lll?** Fill in the bubble under the answer that begins with the sound **lll.** (Allow time for the students to fill in their answers.) You should have filled in the second bubble. If you did not, cross out your answer and fill in the second bubble now.

3. Touch row 3. Look at the pictures. Which picture shows an animal that likes to lick? Fill in the bubble under the picture of the animal that likes to lick. (Allow time for the students to fill in their answers.) You should have filled in the third bubble. If you did not, cross out your answer and fill in the third bubble now.

4. Touch row 4. Look at the answers. Which answer is the word **sand?** Fill in the bubble under the word **sand.** (Allow time for the students to fill in their answers.) You should have filled in the third bubble. If you did not, cross out your answer and fill in the third bubble now.

It's time to stop. You did a good job filling in the bubbles. **(Collect the test pages.)**

Lesson 75

Name ____________________ Date ____________

1

2

far ◯ let ◯ the ◯

3

4

rain ◯ late ◯ sand ◯

(Duplicate the test page for each child and fill in the name and date on each test. Be sure each child has a pencil. Distribute the tests.)

1. Put your finger on row 1. Look at the pictures. Which picture shows a **rat?** Fill in the bubble under the picture of the **rat.** (Allow time for the students to fill in their answers.) You should have filled in the first bubble. If you did not, cross out your answer and fill in the first bubble now.

2. Touch row 2. Look at the letters. Which letter makes the sound **www?** Fill in the bubble under the letter that makes the sound **www.** (Allow time for the students to fill in their answers.) You should have filled in the second bubble. If you did not, cross out your answer and fill in the second bubble now.

3. Touch row 3. Look at the pictures. Which picture shows the place you would see sand? Fill in the bubble under the picture of the place you would see sand. (Allow time for the students to fill in their answers.) You should have filled in the third bubble. If you did not, cross out your answer and fill in the third bubble now.

4. Touch row 4. Look at the answers. Which answer is the word **hand?** Fill in the bubble under the word **hand.** (Allow time for the students to fill in their answers.) You should have filled in the first bubble. If you did not, cross out your answer and fill in the first bubble now.

It's time to stop. You did a good job filling in the bubbles. **(Collect the test pages.)**

Lesson 76

Name ______________________ Date ____________

1

○ ○ ○

2

s w n

○ ○ ○

3

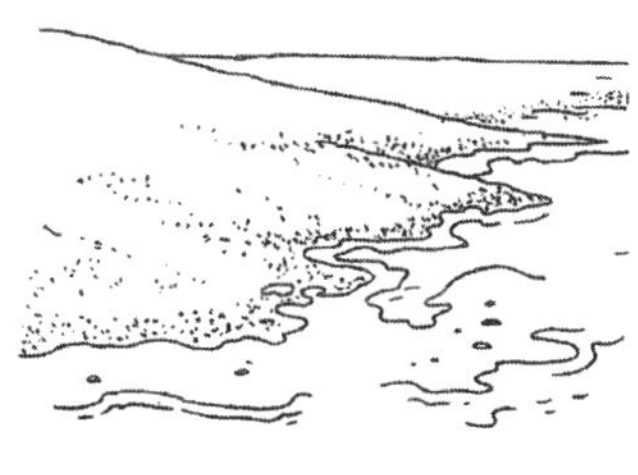

○ ○ ○

4

hand late rain

○ ○ ○

Lesson 77

(Duplicate the test page for each child and fill in the name and date on each test. Be sure each child has a pencil. Distribute the tests.)

1 Put your finger on row 1. Look at the pictures. They show a tie, a phone, and a wig. Which answer has the same beginning sound as **wind?** Fill in the bubble under the answer that has the same beginning sound as **wind.** (Allow time for the students to fill in their answers.) You should have filled in the third bubble. If you did not, cross out your answer and fill in the third bubble now.

2 Touch row 2. Look at the answers. Which answer shows **www aaa?** Fill in the bubble under the answer that shows **www aaa.** (Allow time for the students to fill in their answers.) You should have filled in the first bubble. If you did not, cross out your answer and fill in the first bubble now.

3 Touch row 3. Look at the pictures. Which picture shows a **pig?** Fill in the bubble under the picture of the **pig.** (Allow time for the students to fill in their answers.) You should have filled in the second bubble. If you did not, cross out your answer and fill in the second bubble now.

4 Touch row 4. Look at the answers. Which answer is the word **mail?** Fill in the bubble under the word **mail.** (Allow time for the students to fill in their answers.) You should have filled in the first bubble. If you did not, cross out your answer and fill in the first bubble now.

It's time to stop. You did a good job filling in the bubbles. **(Collect the test pages.)**

Lesson 77

Name ______________________ Date ______________

❶

❷

wa bi it

❸

❹

mail game rain

 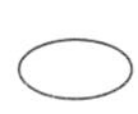 

(Duplicate the test page for each child and fill in the name and date on each test. Be sure each child has a pencil. Distribute the tests.)

1. Put your finger on row 1. Look at the pictures. They show a string, a bow, and a rope. Which answer rhymes with **show?** Fill in the bubble under the answer that rhymes with **show.** (Allow time for the students to fill in their answers.) You should have filled in the second bubble. If you did not, cross out your answer and fill in the second bubble now.

2. Touch row 2. Look at the answers. Two of the answers are the same, and one is different. Which answer is different? Fill in the bubble under the answer that is different. (Allow time for the students to fill in their answers.) You should have filled in the second bubble. If you did not, cross out your answer and fill in the second bubble now.

3. Touch row 3. Look at the pictures. Which picture shows a boat with a sail? Fill in the bubble under the picture of a boat with a sail. (Allow time for the students to fill in their answers.) You should have filled in the first bubble. If you did not, cross out your answer and fill in the first bubble now.

4. Touch row 4. Look at the answers. Which answer is the word **game?** Fill in the bubble under the word **game.** (Allow time for the students to fill in their answers.) You should have filled in the third bubble. If you did not, cross out your answer and fill in the third bubble now.

It's time to stop. You did a good job filling in the bubbles. **(Collect the test pages.)**

Lesson 78

Name ______________________ Date ______________

❶

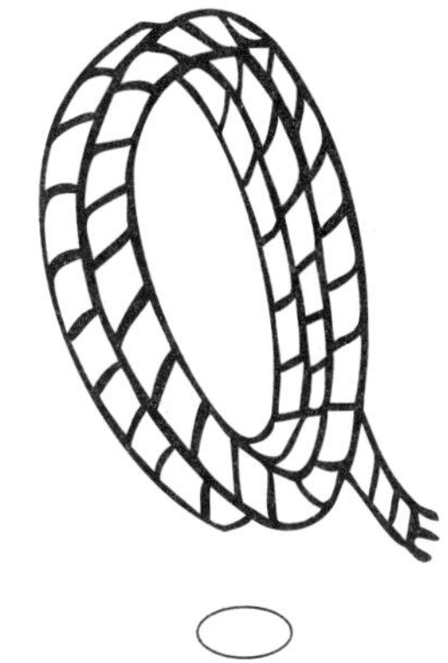

❷

mail | nail | mail

❸

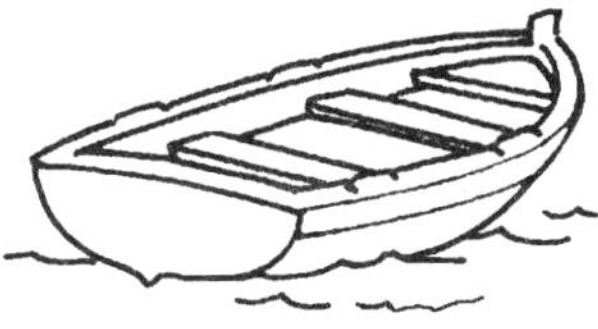

❹

seem | same | game

Lesson 79

(Duplicate the test page for each child and fill in the name and date on each test. Be sure each child has a pencil. Distribute the tests.)

1. Put your finger on row 1. Look at the pictures. Which picture goes with the words *something you mail?* Fill in the bubble under the picture that goes with the words *something you mail.* (Allow time for the students to fill in their answers.) You should have filled in the third bubble. If you did not, cross out your answer and fill in the third bubble now.

2. Touch row 2. Look at the words. Which word begins with the sound **www?** Fill in the bubble under the answer that begins with the sound **www.** (Allow time for the students to fill in their answers.) You should have filled in the first bubble. If you did not, cross out your answer and fill in the first bubble now.

3. Touch row 3. Look at the pictures. Which picture shows a jar with a **lid?** Fill in the bubble under the picture of the jar with a **lid.** (Allow time for the students to fill in their answers.) You should have filled in the first bubble. If you did not, cross out your answer and fill in the first bubble now.

4. Touch row 4. Look at the answers. Which answer is the word **sag?** Fill in the bubble under the word **sag.** (Allow time for the students to fill in their answers.) You should have filled in the second bubble. If you did not, cross out your answer and fill in the second bubble now.

It's time to stop. You did a good job filling in the bubbles. **(Collect the test pages.)**

Lesson 79

Name ______________________ Date ______________

❶

❷ wag sad hit

❸

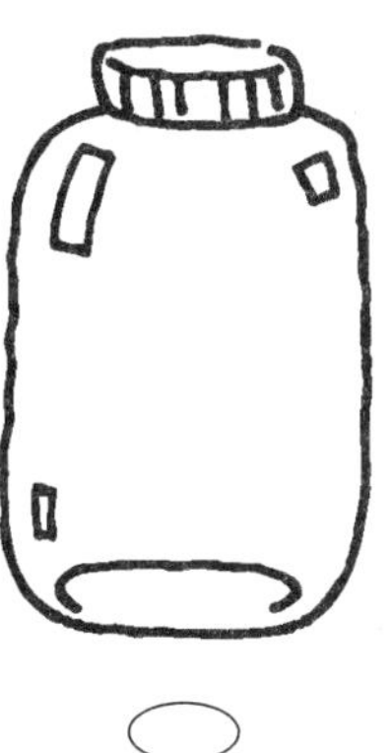

❹ wag sag tag

(Duplicate the test page for each child and fill in the name and date on each test. Be sure each child has a pencil. Distribute the tests.)

Today we are going to do something different. I am going to read a story out loud. Then we will answer some questions about the story. Listen carefully. (Read the story out loud.)

Fresh Fruit

The tree was covered with apples. Ted could not wait to pick some. There was only one problem. He was too short. The apples were up high.

Mom had an idea. She got a ladder. She put it against the tree. Ted climbed the ladder. Mom held it. He picked lots of nice apples.

Now we will answer the questions.

1. Put your finger on row 1. Look at the pictures. Which picture shows what Ted was picking? Fill in the bubble under the picture of the fruit that Ted was picking. (Allow time for the students to fill in their answers.) You should have filled in the second bubble. If you did not, cross out your answer and fill in the second bubble now.

2. Touch row 2. Look at the pictures. What did Ted use to get up the tree? Fill in the bubble under the picture of what Ted used to get up the tree. (Allow time for the students to fill in their answers.) You should have filled in the first bubble. If you did not, cross out your answer and fill in the first bubble now.

It's time to stop. You did a good job filling in the bubbles. **(Collect the test pages.)**

Lesson
80

Name ______________________ Date ______________

1

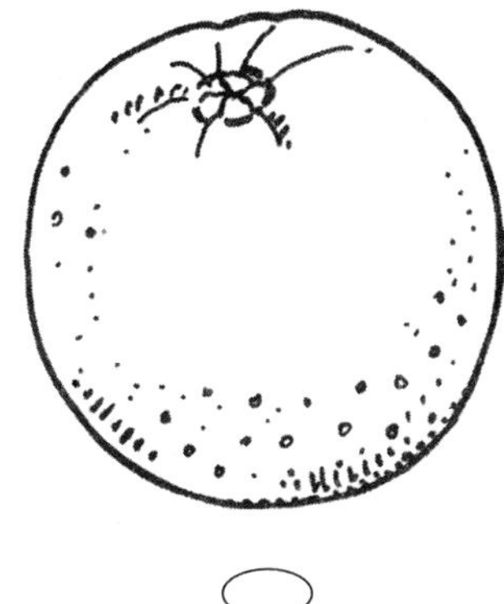

2

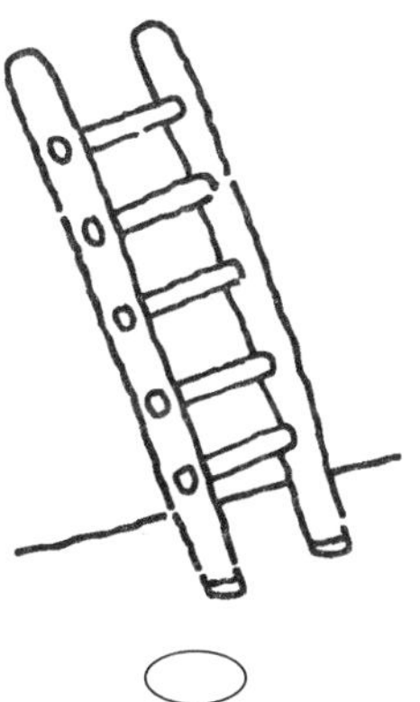

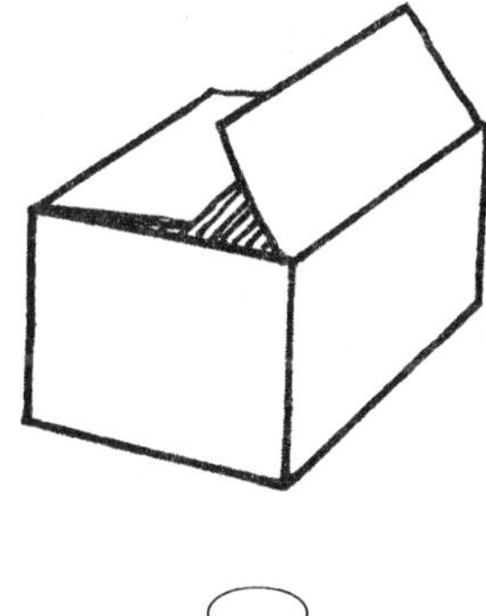

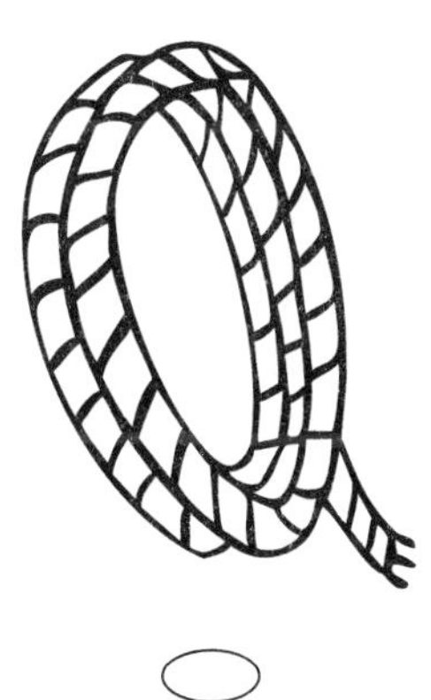

(Duplicate the test page for each child and fill in the name and date on each test. Be sure each child has a pencil. Distribute the tests.)

1 Put your finger on row 1. Look at the answers. Which answer makes the sound **shshsh?** Fill in the bubble under the letter that makes the sound **shshsh.** (Allow time for the students to fill in their answers.) You should have filled in the second bubble. If you did not, cross out your answer and fill in the second bubble now.

2 Touch row 2. Look at the pictures. Which picture goes with the words *Ron can run?* Fill in the bubble under the picture that goes with the words *Ron can run.* (Allow time for the students to fill in their answers.) You should have filled in the first bubble. If you did not, cross out your answer and fill in the first bubble now.

3 Touch row 3. Look at the words. Two of the words are the same and one is different. Which word is different? Fill in the bubble under the word that is different. (Allow time for the students to fill in their answers.) You should have filled in the third bubble. If you did not, cross out your answer and fill in the third bubble now.

4 Touch row 4. Look at the answers. Which answer is the word **tame?** Fill in the bubble under the word **tame.** (Allow time for the students to fill in their answers.) You should have filled in the second bubble. If you did not, cross out your answer and fill in the second bubble now.

It's time to stop. You did a good job filling in the bubbles. **(Collect the test pages.)**

Lesson 81

Name ______________________ Date ______________

1 th ◯ sh ◯ dr ◯

2

3 mill ◯ mill ◯ will ◯

4 rain ◯ tame ◯ will ◯

(Duplicate the test page for each child and fill in the name and date on each test. Be sure each child has a pencil. Distribute the tests.)

1. Put your finger on row 1. Look at the pictures. Which picture shows a **ram?** Fill in the bubble under the picture of the **ram.** (Allow time for the students to fill in their answers.) You should have filled in the first bubble. If you did not, cross out your answer and fill in the first bubble now.

2. Touch row 2. Look at the words. Which word begins with the sound **shshsh?** Fill in the bubble under the answer that begins with the sound **shshsh.** (Allow time for the students to fill in their answers.) You should have filled in the second bubble. If you did not, cross out your answer and fill in the second bubble now.

3. Touch row 3. Look at the words. Which word begins with the sound **www?** Fill in the bubble under the answer that begins with the sound **www.** (Allow time for the students to fill in their answers.) You should have filled in the second bubble. If you did not, cross out your answer and fill in the second bubble now.

4. Touch row 4. Look at the answers. Which answer is the word **little?** Fill in the bubble under the word **little.** (Allow time for the students to fill in their answers.) You should have filled in the third bubble. If you did not, cross out your answer and fill in the third bubble now.

It's time to stop. You did a good job filling in the bubbles. **(Collect the test pages.)**

Lesson 82

Name ______________________ Date ______________

1

2 the ◯ she ◯ ran ◯

3 he ◯ we ◯ me ◯

4 made ◯ let ◯ little ◯

Lesson 83

(Duplicate the test page for each child and fill in the name and date on each test. Be sure each child has a pencil. Distribute the tests.)

1. Put your finger on row 1. Look at the pictures. Which picture shows a **hut?** Fill in the bubble under the picture of the **hut.** (Allow time for the students to fill in their answers.) You should have filled in the third bubble. If you did not, cross out your answer and fill in the third bubble now.

2. Touch row 2. Look at the words. Which word begins with the sound **thththth?** Fill in the bubble under the answer that begins with the sound **thththth.** (Allow time for the students to fill in their answers.) You should have filled in the second bubble. If you did not, cross out your answer and fill in the second bubble now.

3. Touch row 3. Look at the letters. Which letter makes the middle sound you hear in the word **not?** Fill in the bubble under the letter that makes the middle sound in the word **not.** (Allow time for the students to fill in their answers.) You should have filled in the third bubble. If you did not, cross out your answer and fill in the third bubble now.

4. Touch row 4. Look at the answers. Which answer is the word **got?** Fill in the bubble under the word **got.** (Allow time for the students to fill in their answers.) You should have filled in the first bubble. If you did not, cross out your answer and fill in the first bubble now.

It's time to stop. You did a good job filling in the bubbles. **(Collect the test pages.)**

Lesson 83

Name ______________________ Date ______________

1

○ ○ ○

2 same ○ that ○ feet ○

3 a ○ i ○ o ○

4 got ○ not ○ get ○

(Duplicate the test page for each child and fill in the name and date on each test. Be sure each child has a pencil. Distribute the tests.)

1. Touch row 1. Look at the pictures. Which picture shows something little? Fill in the bubble under the picture of something little. (Allow time for the students to fill in their answers.) You should have filled in the first bubble. If you did not, cross out your answer and fill in the first bubble now.

2. Touch row 2. Look at the words. Which word rhymes with **as?** Fill in the bubble under the word that rhymes with **as.** (Allow time for the students to fill in their answers.) You should have filled in the second bubble. If you did not, cross out your answer and fill in the second bubble now.

3. Touch row 3. Look at the answers. Which answer shows **nnn ooo t?** Fill in the bubble under the answer that shows **nnn ooo t.** (Allow time for the students to fill in their answers.) You should have filled in the first bubble. If you did not, cross out your answer and fill in the first bubble now.

4. Touch row 4. Look at the answers. Which answer is the word **shack?** Fill in the bubble under the word **shack.** (Allow time for the students to fill in their answers.) You should have filled in the third bubble. If you did not, cross out your answer and fill in the third bubble now.

It's time to stop. You did a good job filling in the bubbles. **(Collect the test pages.)**

Lesson 84

Name ______________________ Date ______________

❶

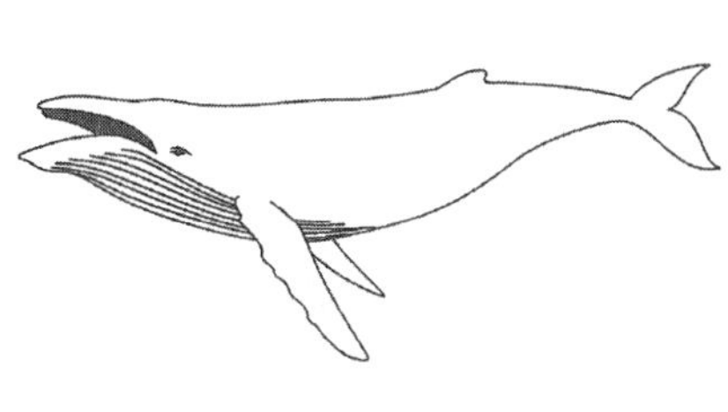

○ ○ ○

❷ sad ○ has ○ hit ○

❸ n o t ○ t o n ○ o n t ○

❹ make ○ little ○ shack ○

Lesson 85

(Duplicate the test page for each child and fill in the name and date on each test. Be sure each child has a pencil. Distribute the tests.)

1. Put your finger on row 1. Look at the pictures. Which picture shows a **shack?** Fill in the bubble under the picture of the **shack.** (Allow time for the students to fill in their answers.) You should have filled in the third bubble. If you did not, cross out your answer and fill in the third bubble now.

2. Touch row 2. Look at the pictures. They show a clam, a fish, and a seal. Which one ends with the sound **shshsh?** Fill in the bubble under the picture that ends with the sound **shshsh.** (Allow time for the students to fill in their answers.) You should have filled in the second bubble. If you did not, cross out your answer and fill in the second bubble now.

3. Touch row 3. Look at the answers. Which word has the same middle sound as **dot?** Fill in the bubble under the answer that has the same middle sound as **dot.** (Allow time for the students to fill in their answers.) You should have filled in the third bubble. If you did not, cross out your answer and fill in the third bubble now.

4. Touch row 4. Look at the answers. Which answer is the word **did?** Fill in the bubble under the word **did.** (Allow time for the students to fill in their answers.) You should have filled in the first bubble. If you did not, cross out your answer and fill in the first bubble now.

It's time to stop. You did a good job filling in the bubbles. **(Collect the test pages.)**

Lesson
85

Name ______________________ Date ______________

1

○ ○ ○

2

○ ○ ○

3 meat let got

○ ○ ○

4 did dad rid

○ ○ ○

Lesson 86

(Duplicate the test page for each child and fill in the name and date on each test. Be sure each child has a pencil. Distribute the tests.)

1. Put your finger on row 1. Look at the pictures. Which picture shows an animal with big ears? Fill in the bubble under the picture of the animal with big ears. (Allow time for the students to fill in their answers.) You should have filled in the third bubble. If you did not, cross out your answer and fill in the third bubble now.

2. Touch row 2. Look at the answers. Which answer shows **iii fff?** Fill in the bubble under the answer that shows **iii fff.** (Allow time for the students to fill in their answers.) You should have filled in the second bubble. If you did not, cross out your answer and fill in the second bubble now.

3. Touch row 3. Look at the words. Two of the words are the same and one is different. Which word is different? Fill in the bubble under the word that is different. (Allow time for the students to fill in their answers.) You should have filled in the first bubble. If you did not, cross out your answer and fill in the first bubble now.

4. Touch row 4. Look at the answers. Which answer is the word **hears?** Fill in the bubble under the word **hears.** (Allow time for the students to fill in their answers.) You should have filled in the first bubble. If you did not, cross out your answer and fill in the first bubble now.

It's time to stop. You did a good job filling in the bubbles. **(Collect the test pages.)**

Lesson
86

Name ______________________ Date ______________

1

2 it if in

3 runs run run

4 hears that sand

Lesson 87

(Duplicate the test page for each child and fill in the name and date on each test. Be sure each child has a pencil. Distribute the tests.)

1. Put your finger on row 1. Look at the pictures. Which picture goes with the words *a wet dog?* Fill in the bubble under the picture that goes with the words *a wet dog.* (Allow time for the students to fill in their answers.) You should have filled in the second bubble. If you did not, cross out your answer and fill in the second bubble now.

2. Touch row 2. Look at the words. Which word ends with the sound **lll?** Fill in the bubble under the answer that ends with the sound **lll.** (Allow time for the students to fill in their answers.) You should have filled in the first bubble. If you did not, cross out your answer and fill in the first bubble now.

3. Touch row 3. Look at the answers. Which answer shows **uuu nnn sss?** Fill in the bubble under the answer that shows **uuu nnn sss.** (Allow time for the students to fill in their answers.) You should have filled in the second bubble. If you did not, cross out your answer and fill in the second bubble now.

4. Touch row 4. Look at the answers. Which answer is the word **suns?** Fill in the bubble under the word **suns.** (Allow time for the students to fill in their answers.) You should have filled in the third bubble. If you did not, cross out your answer and fill in the third bubble now.

It's time to stop. You did a good job filling in the bubbles. **(Collect the test pages.)**

Lesson 87

Name ______________________ Date ______________

1

2 tall it sack

3 sun uns nus

4 seen runs suns

(Duplicate the test page for each child and fill in the name and date on each test. Be sure each child has a pencil. Distribute the tests.)

1. Put your finger on row 1. Look at the answers. Which answer shows **III?** Fill in the bubble under the answer that shows **III. (Allow time for the students to fill in their answers.)** You should have filled in the first bubble. If you did not, cross out your answer and fill in the first bubble now.

2. Touch row 2. Look at the pictures. Which picture shows a **diiishshsh?** Fill in the bubble under the picture of the **diiishshsh. (Allow time for the students to fill in their answers.)** You should have filled in the second bubble. If you did not, cross out your answer and fill in the second bubble now.

3. Touch row 3. Look at the pictures. Which picture shows a **monkey?** Fill in the bubble under the picture of the **monkey. (Allow time for the students to fill in their answers.)** You should have filled in the first bubble. If you did not, cross out your answer and fill in the first bubble now.

4. Touch row 4. Look at the answers. Which answer is the word **wins?** Fill in the bubble under the word **wins. (Allow time for the students to fill in their answers.)** You should have filled in the third bubble. If you did not, cross out your answer and fill in the third bubble now.

It's time to stop. You did a good job filling in the bubbles. **(Collect the test pages.)**

Lesson 88

Name ______________________ Date ______________

1. I t l

2. 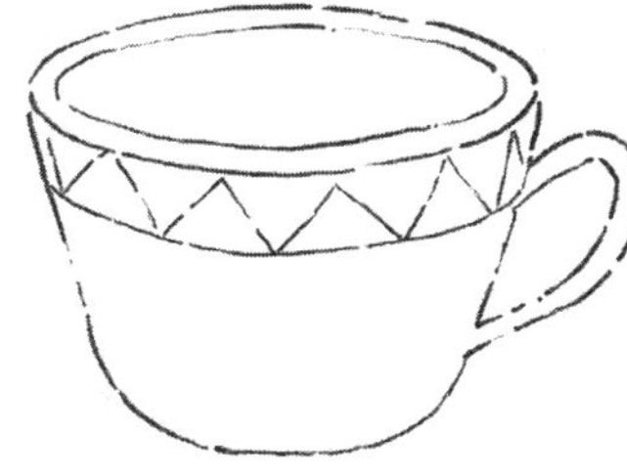 

3.  

4. runs suns wins

(Duplicate the test page for each child and fill in the name and date on each test. Be sure each child has a pencil. Distribute the tests.)

1 Put your finger on row 1. Look at the pictures. Which picture goes with the words *at the beach?* Fill in the bubble under the picture that goes with the words *at the beach.* (Allow time for the students to fill in their answers.) You should have filled in the third bubble. If you did not, cross out your answer and fill in the third bubble now.

2 Touch row 2. Look at the answers. Which answer shows the words **is hot?** Fill in the bubble under the answer that shows **is hot.** (Allow time for the students to fill in their answers.) You should have filled in the second bubble. If you did not, cross out your answer and fill in the second bubble now.

3 Touch row 3. Look at the words. Two of the words are the same and one is different. Which word is different? Fill in the bubble under the word that is different. (Allow time for the students to fill in their answers.) You should have filled in the third bubble. If you did not, cross out your answer and fill in the third bubble now.

4 Touch row 4. Look at the answers. Which answer is the word **said?** Fill in the bubble under the word **said.** (Allow time for the students to fill in their answers.) You should have filled in the first bubble. If you did not, cross out your answer and fill in the first bubble now.

It's time to stop. You did a good job filling in the bubbles. **(Collect the test pages.)**

Lesson 89

Name ______________________ Date ______________

1

2 in the — is hot — run at

3 dish — dish — wish

4 said — will — hats

Lesson 90

(Duplicate the test page for each child and fill in the name and date on each test. Be sure each child has a pencil. Distribute the tests.)

1. Put your finger on row 1. Look at the pictures. Which picture shows some **tacks?** Fill in the bubble under the picture of the **tacks.** **(Allow time for the students to fill in their answers.)** You should have filled in the second bubble. If you did not, cross out your answer and fill in the second bubble now.

2. Touch row 2. Look at the words. Two of the words are the same and one is different. Which word is different? Fill in the bubble under the word that is different. **(Allow time for the students to fill in their answers.)** You should have filled in the second bubble. If you did not, cross out your answer and fill in the second bubble now.

3. Touch row 3. Look at the pictures. Which picture goes with the words *something you can shut?* Fill in the bubble under the picture that goes with the words *something you can shut.* **(Allow time for the students to fill in their answers.)** You should have filled in the first bubble. If you did not, cross out your answer and fill in the first bubble now.

4. Touch row 4. Look at the answers. Which answer is the word **with?** Fill in the bubble under the word **with.** **(Allow time for the students to fill in their answers.)** You should have filled in the third bubble. If you did not, cross out your answer and fill in the third bubble now.

It's time to stop. You did a good job filling in the bubbles. **(Collect the test pages.)**

Lesson 90

Name ____________________ Date ____________

1

2 sad said sad

3

4 sacks said with

(Duplicate the test page for each child and fill in the name and date on each test. Be sure each child has a pencil. Distribute the tests.)

1 Put your finger on row 1. Look at the pictures. Which picture shows a girl with tears? Fill in the bubble under the picture of the girl with tears. (Allow time for the students to fill in their answers.) You should have filled in the second bubble. If you did not, cross out your answer and fill in the second bubble now.

2 Touch row 2. Look at the answers. Which answer shows **wwwiiinnn?** Fill in the bubble under the answer that shows **wwwiiinnn.** (Allow time for the students to fill in their answers.) You should have filled in the first bubble. If you did not, cross out your answer and fill in the first bubble now.

3 Touch row 3. Look at the answers. Two of the answers are the same, and one is different. Which answer is different? Fill in the bubble under the answer that is different. (Allow time for the students to fill in their answers.) You should have filled in the first bubble. If you did not, cross out your answer and fill in the first bubble now.

4 Touch row 4. Look at the answers. Which answer is the word **tears?** Fill in the bubble under the word **tears.** (Allow time for the students to fill in their answers.) You should have filled in the third bubble. If you did not, cross out your answer and fill in the third bubble now.

It's time to stop. You did a good job filling in the bubbles. **(Collect the test pages.)**

Lesson 91

Name ______________________ Date ______________

1

2 win fin tin

3 now not not

4 tames teams tears

(Duplicate the test page for each child and fill in the name and date on each test. Be sure each child has a pencil. Distribute the tests.)

1. Put your finger on row 1. Look at the pictures. Which picture goes with the words *something you kick?* Fill in the bubble under the picture that goes with the words *something you kick.* (Allow time for the students to fill in their answers.) You should have filled in the first bubble. If you did not, cross out your answer and fill in the first bubble now.

2. Touch row 2. Look at the letters. Which letter makes the sound **k?** Fill in the bubble under the letter that makes the sound **k.** (Allow time for the students to fill in their answers.) You should have filled in the third bubble. If you did not, cross out your answer and fill in the third bubble now.

3. Touch row 3. Look at the pictures. Which picture shows a **rake?** Fill in the bubble under the picture of the **rake.** (Allow time for the students to fill in their answers.) You should have filled in the second bubble. If you did not, cross out your answer and fill in the second bubble now.

4. Touch row 4. Look at the answers. Which answer is the word **games?** Fill in the bubble under the word **games.** (Allow time for the students to fill in their answers.) You should have filled in the third bubble. If you did not, cross out your answer and fill in the third bubble now.

It's time to stop. You did a good job filling in the bubbles. **(Collect the test pages.)**

Lesson 92

Name ____________________ Date ____________

❶

❷ t f k

❸

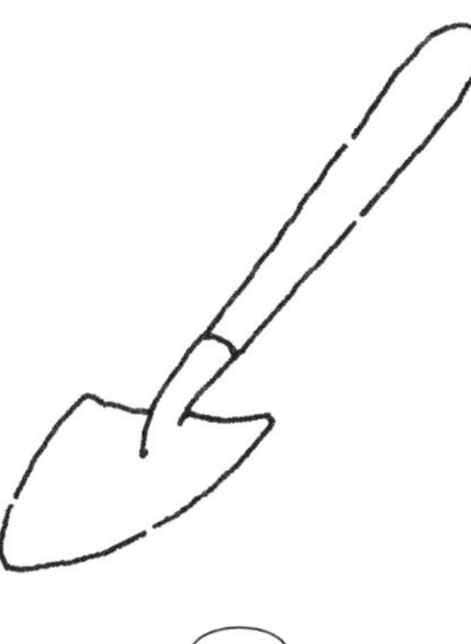

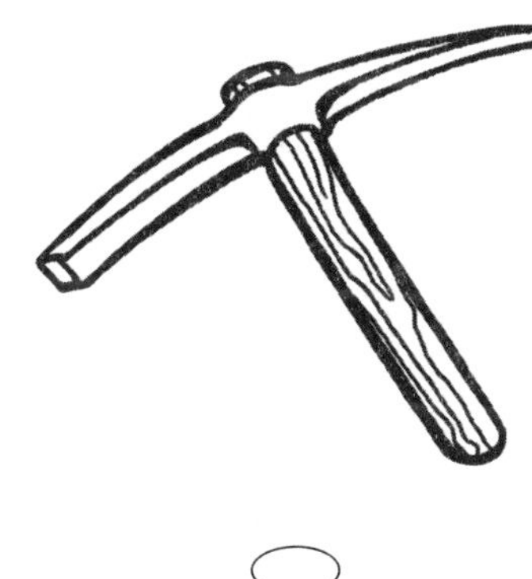

❹ tames names games

(Duplicate the test page for each child and fill in the name and date on each test. Be sure each child has a pencil. Distribute the tests.)

1 Put your finger on row 1. Look at the words. Which word begins with the sound **k?** Fill in the bubble under the answer that begins with the sound **k.** (Allow time for the students to fill in their answers.) You should have filled in the second bubble. If you did not, cross out your answer and fill in the second bubble now.

2 Touch row 2. Look at the answers. Which answer shows **cooowww?** Fill in the bubble under the answer that shows **cooowww.** (Allow time for the students to fill in their answers.) You should have filled in the third bubble. If you did not, cross out your answer and fill in the third bubble now.

3 Touch row 3. Look at the pictures. Which picture goes with the words *little cat?* Fill in the bubble under the picture that goes with the words *little cat.* (Allow time for the students to fill in their answers.) You should have filled in the first bubble. If you did not, cross out your answer and fill in the first bubble now.

4 Touch row 4. Look at the answers. Which answer is the word **this?** Fill in the bubble under the word **this.** (Allow time for the students to fill in their answers.) You should have filled in the second bubble. If you did not, cross out your answer and fill in the second bubble now.

It's time to stop. You did a good job filling in the bubbles. **(Collect the test pages.)**

Lesson 93

Name ______________________ Date ______________

1. tick ◯ kick ◯ sick ◯

2. map ◯ hit ◯ cow ◯

3.  ◯  ◯  ◯

4. said ◯ this ◯ will ◯

(Duplicate the test page for each child and fill in the name and date on each test. Be sure each child has a pencil. Distribute the tests.)

1. Put your finger on row 1. Look at the letters. Which letter makes the last sound you hear in the word **ink?** Fill in the bubble under the letter that makes the last sound in the word **ink.** (Allow time for the students to fill in their answers.) You should have filled in the third bubble. If you did not, cross out your answer and fill in the third bubble now.

2. Touch row 2. Look at the pictures. Which picture shows a little fish on top of a big fish? Fill in the bubble under the picture of the little fish on top of the big fish. (Allow time for the students to fill in their answers.) You should have filled in the second bubble. If you did not, cross out your answer and fill in the second bubble now.

3. Touch row 3. Look at the answers. Which answer shows **lllaaat?** Fill in the bubble under the answer that shows **lllaaat.** (Allow time for the students to fill in their answers.) You should have filled in the third bubble. If you did not, cross out your answer and fill in the third bubble now. (**NOTE:** THIS IS THE FIRST TIME WE ARE USING NONSENSE WORDS.)

4. Touch row 4. Look at the answers. Which answer is the word **shut?** Fill in the bubble under the word **shut.** (Allow time for the students to fill in their answers.) You should have filled in the first bubble. If you did not, cross out your answer and fill in the first bubble now.

It's time to stop. You did a good job filling in the bubbles. **(Collect the test pages.)**

Lesson 94

Name ______________________________ Date ____________________

1 l ◯ h ◯ k ◯

2  ◯ ◯  ◯

3 wak ◯ tal ◯ lat ◯

4 shut ◯ late ◯ wish ◯

Lesson 95

(Duplicate the test page for each child and fill in the name and date on each test. Be sure each child has a pencil. Distribute the tests.)

1. Put your finger on row 1. Look at the pictures. Which picture shows a **gate?** Fill in the bubble under the picture of the **gate.** (Allow time for the students to fill in their answers.) You should have filled in the first bubble. If you did not, cross out your answer and fill in the first bubble now.

2. Touch row 2. Look at the answers. Which answer shows **shshsh?** Fill in the bubble under the answer that shows **shshsh.** (Allow time for the students to fill in their answers.) You should have filled in the second bubble. If you did not, cross out your answer and fill in the second bubble now.

3. Touch row 3. Look at the pictures. Which picture shows a **dollar?** Fill in the bubble under the picture of the **dollar.** (Allow time for the students to fill in their answers.) You should have filled in the third bubble. If you did not, cross out your answer and fill in the third bubble now.

4. Touch row 4. Look at the answers. Which answer is the word **was?** Fill in the bubble under the word **was.** (Allow time for the students to fill in their answers.) You should have filled in the first bubble. If you did not, cross out your answer and fill in the first bubble now.

It's time to stop. You did a good job filling in the bubbles. **(Collect the test pages.)**

Lesson 95

Name ______________________ Date ______________

❶

◯ ◯ ◯

❷

st ◯ sh ◯ sk ◯

❸

◯ ◯ ◯

❹

was ◯ fat ◯ mad ◯

Lesson 96

(Duplicate the test page for each child and fill in the name and date on each test. Be sure each child has a pencil. Distribute the tests.)

1 Put your finger on row 1. Listen to this sentence. "The fish ate a rock." Which picture shows what the fish ate? Fill in the bubble under the picture that shows what the fish ate. (Allow time for the students to fill in their answers.) You should have filled in the third bubble. If you did not, cross out your answer and fill in the third bubble now.

2 Touch row 2. Look at the answers. Which answer has quotation marks around it? Fill in the bubble under the answer that has quotation marks around it. (Allow time for the students to fill in their answers.) You should have filled in the first bubble. If you did not, cross out your answer and fill in the first bubble now.

3 Touch row 3. Look at the answers. Two of the answers are the same, and one is different. Which answer is different? Fill in the bubble under the answer that is different. (Allow time for the students to fill in their answers.) You should have filled in the second bubble. If you did not, cross out your answer and fill in the second bubble now.

4 Touch row 4. Look at the answers. Which answer is the word **feel?** Fill in the bubble under the word **feel.** (Allow time for the students to fill in their answers.) You should have filled in the first bubble. If you did not, cross out your answer and fill in the first bubble now.

It's time to stop. You did a good job filling in the bubbles. **(Collect the test pages.)**

Lesson 96

Name ______________________ Date ______________

1   

2 "gate" hate late

3 lock rock lock

4 feel fill fish

Lesson 97

(Duplicate the test page for each child and fill in the name and date on each test. Be sure each child has a pencil. Distribute the tests.)

1. Put your finger on row 1. Look at the pictures. Which picture goes with the words *not a cat?* Fill in the bubble under the picture that goes with the words *not a cat.* (Allow time for the students to fill in their answers.) You should have filled in the second bubble. If you did not, cross out your answer and fill in the second bubble now.

2. Touch row 2. Look at the answers. Which answer is the sentence *She is?* Fill in the bubble under the sentence *She is.* (Allow time for the students to fill in their answers.) You should have filled in the first bubble. If you did not, cross out your answer and fill in the first bubble now.

3. Touch row 3. Look at the words. Which picture rhymes with **he?** Fill in the bubble under the picture that rhymes with **he.** (Allow time for the students to fill in their answers.) You should have filled in the second bubble. If you did not, cross out your answer and fill in the second bubble now.

4. Touch row 4. Look at the answers. Which answer is the word **nod?** Fill in the bubble under the word **nod.** (Allow time for the students to fill in their answers.) You should have filled in the third bubble. If you did not, cross out your answer and fill in the third bubble now.

It's time to stop. You did a good job filling in the bubbles. **(Collect the test pages.)**

Lesson 97

Name ______________________ Date ______________

❶

○ ○ ○

❷ She is. I am. He was.

○ ○ ○

❸ him she his

○ ○ ○

❹ not don nod

○ ○ ○

Lesson 98

(Duplicate the test page for each child and fill in the name and date on each test. Be sure each child has a pencil. Distribute the tests.)

1. Put your finger on row 1. Look at the letters. Which letter makes the last sound you hear in the word **no?** Fill in the bubble under the letter that makes the last sound in the word **no.** **(Allow time for the students to fill in their answers.)** You should have filled in the first bubble. If you did not, cross out your answer and fill in the first bubble now.

2. Touch row 2. Look at the answers. Which answer is a question mark? Fill in the bubble under the question mark. **(Allow time for the students to fill in their answers.)** You should have filled in the second bubble. If you did not, cross out your answer and fill in the second bubble now.

3. Touch row 3. Look at the pictures. Which picture goes with the words *something children like to hug?* Fill in the bubble under the picture that goes with the words *something children like to hug.* **(Allow time for the students to fill in their answers.)** You should have filled in the first bubble. If you did not, cross out your answer and fill in the first bubble now.

4. Touch row 4. Look at the answers. Which answer is the word **those?** Fill in the bubble under the word **those.** **(Allow time for the students to fill in their answers.)** You should have filled in the third bubble. If you did not, cross out your answer and fill in the third bubble now.

It's time to stop. You did a good job filling in the bubbles. **(Collect the test pages.)**

Lesson 98

Name ______________________ Date ______________

❶ o ◯ a ◯ e ◯

❷ . ◯ ? ◯ “ ◯

❸

◯

◯

◯

❹ that ◯ this ◯ those ◯

(Duplicate the test page for each child and fill in the name and date on each test. Be sure each child has a pencil. Distribute the tests.)

1. Put your finger on row 1. Look at the pictures. Which picture shows **cakes?** Fill in the bubble under the picture of **cakes.** (Allow time for the students to fill in their answers.) You should have filled in the third bubble. If you did not, cross out your answer and fill in the third bubble now.

2. Touch row 2. Look at the words. Which word ends with the sound **thththth?** Fill in the bubble under the answer that ends with the sound **thththth.** (Allow time for the students to fill in their answers.) You should have filled in the second bubble. If you did not, cross out your answer and fill in the second bubble now.

3. Touch row 3. Look at the pictures. Which picture shows a **cat sitting?** Fill in the bubble under the picture of the **cat sitting.** (Allow time for the students to fill in their answers.) You should have filled in the third bubble. If you did not, cross out your answer and fill in the third bubble now.

4. Touch row 4. Look at the answers. Which answer is the word **go?** Fill in the bubble under the word **go.** (Allow time for the students to fill in their answers.) You should have filled in the first bubble. If you did not, cross out your answer and fill in the first bubble now.

It's time to stop. You did a good job filling in the bubbles. **(Collect the test pages.)**

Name ____________________ Date ____________

❶

○ ○ ○

❷

that ○

with ○

hit ○

❸

○ ○ ○

❹

go ○

no ○

so ○

(Duplicate the test page for each child and fill in the name and date on each test. Be sure each child has a pencil. Distribute the tests.)

You have seen this before. I am going to read a story out loud. Then we will answer some questions about the story. Listen carefully. (Read the story out loud.)

A Pretty Bird

Jeff heard the bird. It had a pretty song. The bird was on a bush in the swamp.

The bird was almost all black. It had a little spot of color on its wing. Jeff asked Mom what kind of bird it was. She said it was a red-winged blackbird.

Now we will answer the questions.

1. Put your finger on row 1. Look at the pictures. They show a forest, a desert, and a swamp. Which picture shows where Jeff saw the bird? Fill in the bubble under the answer that shows where Jeff saw the bird. (Allow time for the students to fill in their answers.) You should have filled in the third bubble. If you did not, cross out your answer and fill in the third bubble now.

2. Touch row 2. Look at the pictures. Which picture shows the bird that Jeff probably saw? Fill in the bubble under the picture of the bird Jeff probably saw. (Allow time for the students to fill in their answers.) You should have filled in the second bubble. If you did not, cross out your answer and fill in the second bubble now.

It's time to stop. You did a good job filling in the bubbles. Let's go over your answers. **(Review the answers with the children. Collect the test pages.)**

Lesson 100

Name ____________________ Date ____________

1

2

(Duplicate the test page for each child and fill in the name and date on each test. Be sure each child has a pencil. Distribute the tests.)

1. Put your finger on row 1. Look at the pictures. Which picture goes with the words *a cat and a kitten?* Fill in the bubble under the picture that goes with the words *a cat and a kitten.* (Allow time for the students to fill in their answers.) You should have filled in the second bubble. If you did not, cross out your answer and fill in the second bubble now.

2. Touch row 2. Look at the answers. Which answer shows **ooo vvv?** Fill in the bubble under the answer that shows **ooo vvv.** (Allow time for the students to fill in their answers.) You should have filled in the first bubble. If you did not, cross out your answer and fill in the first bubble now.

3. Touch row 3. Look at the answers. Which answer has the most letters? Fill in the bubble under the answer with the most letters. (Allow time for the students to fill in their answers.) You should have filled in the third bubble. If you did not, cross out your answer and fill in the third bubble now.

4. Touch row 4. Look at the answers. Which answer is the word **for?** Fill in the bubble under the word **for.** (Allow time for the students to fill in their answers.) You should have filled in the second bubble. If you did not, cross out your answer and fill in the second bubble now.

It's time to stop. You did a good job filling in the bubbles. (**Collect the test pages.)**

Name ______________________ Date ______________

1

○ ○ ○

2 of ○ in ○ at ○

3 hit ○ this ○ those ○

4 far ○ for ○ nor ○

Lesson 102

(Duplicate the test page for each child and fill in the name and date on each test. Be sure each child has a pencil. Distribute the tests.)

1. Put your finger on row 1. Look at the letters. Which letter makes the sound **vvv?** Fill in the bubble under the letter that makes the sound **vvv.** **(Allow time for the students to fill in their answers.)** You should have filled in the third bubble. If you did not, cross out your answer and fill in the third bubble now.

2. Touch row 2. Look at the pictures. Which picture goes with the words *an old car?* Fill in the bubble under the picture that goes with the words *an old car.* **(Allow time for the students to fill in their answers.)** You should have filled in the third bubble. If you did not, cross out your answer and fill in the third bubble now.

3. Touch row 3. Look at the words. Which word has the same middle sound as **make?** Fill in the bubble under the answer that has the same middle sound as **make.** **(Allow time for the students to fill in their answers.)** You should have filled in the second bubble. If you did not, cross out your answer and fill in the second bubble now.

4. Touch row 4. Look at the answers. Which answer is the word **those?** Fill in the bubble under the word **those.** **(Allow time for the students to fill in their answers.)** You should have filled in the first bubble. If you did not, cross out your answer and fill in the first bubble now.

It's time to stop. You did a good job filling in the bubbles. **(Collect the test pages.)**

Lesson 102

Name ____________________ Date ____________

1. r ◯ m ◯ v ◯

2. 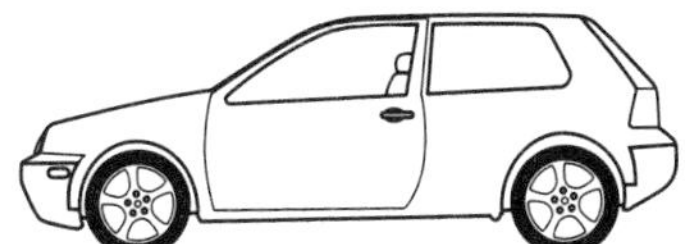 ◯ ◯  ◯

3. with ◯ save ◯ now ◯

4. those ◯ that ◯ this ◯

Lesson 103

(Duplicate the test page for each child and fill in the name and date on each test. Be sure each child has a pencil. Distribute the tests.)

1. Put your finger on row 1. Look at the words. Which word has the sound **vvv?** Fill in the bubble under the answer that has the sound **vvv.** (Allow time for the students to fill in their answers.) You should have filled in the first bubble. If you did not, cross out your answer and fill in the first bubble now.

2. Touch row 2. Look at the pictures. Which picture shows a boy holding a hat? Fill in the bubble under the picture of the boy holding a hat. (Allow time for the students to fill in their answers.) You should have filled in the second bubble. If you did not, cross out your answer and fill in the second bubble now.

3. Touch row 3. Look at the words. Two of the words rhyme and one does not. Which word does NOT rhyme with the others? Fill in the bubble under the word that does NOT rhyme with the others. (Allow time for the students to fill in their answers.) You should have filled in the third bubble. If you did not, cross out your answer and fill in the third bubble now.

4. Touch row 4. Look at the answers. Which answer is the word **sold?** Fill in the bubble under the word **sold.** (Allow time for the students to fill in their answers.) You should have filled in the third bubble. If you did not, cross out your answer and fill in the third bubble now.

It's time to stop. You did a good job filling in the bubbles. **(Collect the test pages.)**

Lesson 103

Name ______________________ Date ______________

1 have ○ ham ○ hat ○

2  ○  ○  ○

3 he ○ she ○ or ○

4 rock ○ sat ○ sold ○

(Duplicate the test page for each child and fill in the name and date on each test. Be sure each child has a pencil. Distribute the tests.)

1. Put your finger on row 1. Look at the pictures. Which picture shows some rocks? Fill in the bubble under the picture of some rocks. (Allow time for the students to fill in their answers.) You should have filled in the second bubble. If you did not, cross out your answer and fill in the second bubble now.

2. Touch row 2. Look at the words. Two of the words BEGIN with the same sound and one is different. Which word begins with a different sound? Fill in the bubble under the word that begins with a different sound. (Allow time for the students to fill in their answers.) You should have filled in the first bubble. If you did not, cross out your answer and fill in the first bubble now.

3. Touch row 3. Look at the pictures. Which picture shows the smallest sack? Fill in the bubble under the picture that shows the smallest sack. (Allow time for the students to fill in their answers.) You should have filled in the third bubble. If you did not, cross out your answer and fill in the third bubble now.

4. Touch row 4. Look at the answers. Which answer is the word **gave?** Fill in the bubble under the word **gave.** (Allow time for the students to fill in their answers.) You should have filled in the second bubble. If you did not, cross out your answer and fill in the second bubble now.

It's time to stop. You did a good job filling in the bubbles. **(Collect the test pages.)**

Lesson 104

Name ______________________ Date ______________

1

2

she the those

3

4

give gave save

Lesson 105

(Duplicate the test page for each child and fill in the name and date on each test. Be sure each child has a pencil. Distribute the tests.)

1. Put your finger on row 1. Look at the pictures. Which picture shows something used for shaving? Fill in the bubble under the picture of something used for shaving. (Allow time for the students to fill in their answers.) You should have filled in the first bubble. If you did not, cross out your answer and fill in the first bubble now.

2. Touch row 2. Look at the letters. Which letter makes the first sound you hear in the word **old?** Fill in the bubble under the letter that makes the first sound in the word **old.** (Allow time for the students to fill in their answers.) You should have filled in the second bubble. If you did not, cross out your answer and fill in the second bubble now.

3. Touch row 3. Look at the answers. Two of the answers are the same, and one is different. Which answer is different? Fill in the bubble under the answer that is different. (Allow time for the students to fill in their answers.) You should have filled in the third bubble. If you did not, cross out your answer and fill in the third bubble now.

4. Touch row 4. Look at the answers. Which answer is the word **shave?** Fill in the bubble under the word **shave.** (Allow time for the students to fill in their answers.) You should have filled in the third bubble. If you did not, cross out your answer and fill in the third bubble now.

It's time to stop. You did a good job filling in the bubbles. **(Collect the test pages.)**

Lesson 105

Name ______________________ Date ______________

1

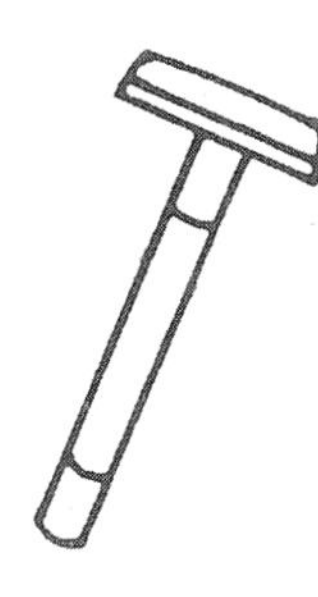

2 a o i

3 hug hug hugs

4 save have shave

(Duplicate the test page for each child and fill in the name and date on each test. Be sure each child has a pencil. Distribute the tests.)

1. Put your finger on row 1. Look at the pictures. Which picture shows a **nose?** Fill in the bubble under the picture of the **nose. (Allow time for the students to fill in their answers.)** You should have filled in the second bubble. If you did not, cross out your answer and fill in the second bubble now.

2. Touch row 2. Look at the words. Which word rhymes with **boat?** Fill in the bubble under the word that rhymes with **boat. (Allow time for the students to fill in their answers.)** You should have filled in the third bubble. If you did not, cross out your answer and fill in the third bubble now.

3. Touch row 3. Look at the pictures. Which picture goes with the words *on your feet?* Fill in the bubble under the picture that goes with the words *on your feet.* **(Allow time for the students to fill in their answers.)** You should have filled in the first bubble. If you did not, cross out your answer and fill in the first bubble now.

4. Touch row 4. Look at the answers. Which answer is the word **need?** Fill in the bubble under the word **need. (Allow time for the students to fill in their answers.)** You should have filled in the second bubble. If you did not, cross out your answer and fill in the second bubble now.

It's time to stop. You did a good job filling in the bubbles. **(Collect the test pages.)**

Name ______________________ Date ______________

1

○

○

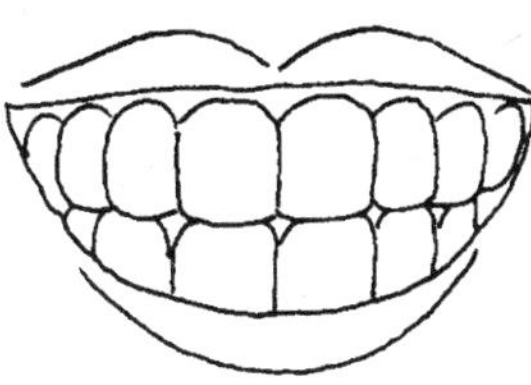
○

2

old ○

rock ○

goat ○

3

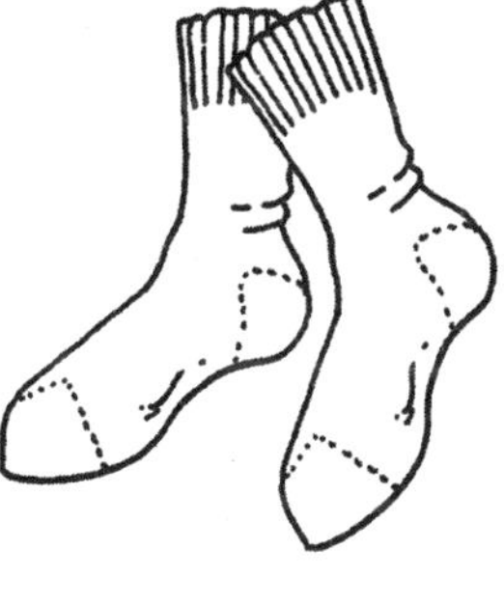
○

○

○

4

seed ○

need ○

feed ○

(Duplicate the test page for each child and fill in the name and date on each test. Be sure each child has a pencil. Distribute the tests.)

1 Put your finger on row 1. Look at the pictures. Which picture goes with the words *a cold day?* Fill in the bubble under the picture that goes with the words *a cold day.* (Allow time for the students to fill in their answers.) You should have filled in the third bubble. If you did not, cross out your answer and fill in the third bubble now.

2 Touch row 2. Look at the answers. Two of the answers are the same, and one is different. Which answer is different? Fill in the bubble under the answer that is different. (Allow time for the students to fill in their answers.) You should have filled in the first bubble. If you did not, cross out your answer and fill in the first bubble now.

3 Touch row 3. Look at the pictures. Which picture shows **goats?** Fill in the bubble under the picture of the **goats.** (Allow time for the students to fill in their answers.) You should have filled in the second bubble. If you did not, cross out your answer and fill in the second bubble now.

4 Touch row 4. Look at the answers. Which answer is the word **was?** Fill in the bubble under the word **was.** (Allow time for the students to fill in their answers.) You should have filled in the first bubble. If you did not, cross out your answer and fill in the first bubble now.

It's time to stop. You did a good job filling in the bubbles. **(Collect the test pages.)**

Lesson 107

Name ______________________ Date ______________

1

2

to so so

3

4

was has wag

Lesson 108

(Duplicate the test page for each child and fill in the name and date on each test. Be sure each child has a pencil. Distribute the tests.)

1. Put your finger on row 1. Look at the letters. Which letter makes the sound **p?** Fill in the bubble under the letter that makes the sound **p.** (Allow time for the students to fill in their answers.) You should have filled in the first bubble. If you did not, cross out your answer and fill in the first bubble now.

2. Touch row 2. Look at the pictures. Which picture shows a **mop?** Fill in the bubble under the picture of the **mop.** (Allow time for the students to fill in their answers.) You should have filled in the second bubble. If you did not, cross out your answer and fill in the second bubble now.

3. Touch row 3. Look at the answers. Two of the answers are the same, and one is different. Which answer is different? Fill in the bubble under the answer that is different. (Allow time for the students to fill in their answers.) You should have filled in the first bubble. If you did not, cross out your answer and fill in the first bubble now.

4. Touch row 4. Look at the answers. Which answer is the word **top?** Fill in the bubble under the word **top.** (Allow time for the students to fill in their answers.) You should have filled in the third bubble. If you did not, cross out your answer and fill in the third bubble now.

It's time to stop. You did a good job filling in the bubbles. **(Collect the test pages.)**

Lesson 108

Name ______________________ Date ______________

❶ p ◯ t ◯ r ◯

❷

◯ ◯

◯

❸ that ◯ hat ◯ hat ◯

❹ dot ◯ map ◯ top ◯

Lesson 109

(Duplicate the test page for each child and fill in the name and date on each test. Be sure each child has a pencil. Distribute the tests.)

1. Put your finger on row 1. Look at the words. Which word begins with the sound **p?** Fill in the bubble under the answer that begins with the sound **p.** (Allow time for the students to fill in their answers.) You should have filled in the second bubble. If you did not, cross out your answer and fill in the second bubble now.

2. Touch row 2. Look at the pictures. Which picture shows a **ship?** Fill in the bubble under the picture of the **ship.** (Allow time for the students to fill in their answers.) You should have filled in the first bubble. If you did not, cross out your answer and fill in the first bubble now.

3. Touch row 3. Look at the answers. Two of the answers are the same, and one is different. Which answer is different? Fill in the bubble under the answer that is different. (Allow time for the students to fill in their answers.) You should have filled in the second bubble. If you did not, cross out your answer and fill in the second bubble now.

4. Touch row 4. Look at the answers. Which answer is the word **down?** Fill in the bubble under the word **down.** (Allow time for the students to fill in their answers.) You should have filled in the third bubble. If you did not, cross out your answer and fill in the third bubble now.

It's time to stop. You did a good job filling in the bubbles. **(Collect the test pages.)**

Lesson 109

Name ______________________ Date ______________

❶ dot ◯ pal ◯ hut ◯

❷  ◯ ◯  ◯

❸ tip ◯ dip ◯ tip ◯

❹ late ◯ said ◯ down ◯

(Duplicate the test page for each child and fill in the name and date on each test. Be sure each child has a pencil. Distribute the tests.)

1. Put your finger on row 1. Look at the pictures. Which picture shows a **log?** Fill in the bubble under the picture of the **log. (Allow time for the students to fill in their answers.)** You should have filled in the third bubble. If you did not, cross out your answer and fill in the third bubble now.

2. Touch row 2. Look at the words. Which word ends with the sound **p?** Fill in the bubble under the answer that ends with the sound **p. (Allow time for the students to fill in their answers.)** You should have filled in the second bubble. If you did not, cross out your answer and fill in the second bubble now.

3. Touch row 3. Look at the answers. Two of the answers are the same, and one is different. Which answer is different? Fill in the bubble under the answer that is different. **(Allow time for the students to fill in their answers.)** You should have filled in the second bubble. If you did not, cross out your answer and fill in the second bubble now.

4. Touch row 4. Look at the answers. Which answer is the word **fog?** Fill in the bubble under the word **fog. (Allow time for the students to fill in their answers.)** You should have filled in the first bubble. If you did not, cross out your answer and fill in the first bubble now.

It's time to stop. You did a good job filling in the bubbles. **(Collect the test pages.)**

Lesson 110

Name ______________________ Date ______________

1

○ ○ ○

2 dot ○ top ○ had ○

3 said ○ sand ○ said ○

4 fog ○ car ○ nod ○

(Duplicate the test page for each child and fill in the name and date on each test. Be sure each child has a pencil. Distribute the tests.)

1. Put your finger on row 1. Look at the pictures. Which picture shows a girl with her hands over her eyes? Fill in the bubble under the picture of the girl with her hands over her eyes. (Allow time for the students to fill in their answers.) You should have filled in the second bubble. If you did not, cross out your answer and fill in the second bubble now.

2. Touch row 2. Look at the letters. Which letter makes the first sound you hear in the word **mop?** Fill in the bubble under the letter that makes the first sound in the word **mop.** (Allow time for the students to fill in their answers.) You should have filled in the third bubble. If you did not, cross out your answer and fill in the third bubble now.

3. Touch row 3. Look at the answers. Two of the answers are the same, and one is different. Which answer is different? Fill in the bubble under the answer that is different. (Allow time for the students to fill in their answers.) You should have filled in the third bubble. If you did not, cross out your answer and fill in the third bubble now.

4. Touch row 4. Look at the answers. Which answer is the word **us?** Fill in the bubble under the word **us.** (Allow time for the students to fill in their answers.) You should have filled in the first bubble. If you did not, cross out your answer and fill in the first bubble now.

It's time to stop. You did a good job filling in the bubbles. **(Collect the test pages.)**

Lesson 111

Name ______________________ Date ______________

1

2 c t m

3 dog dog fog

4 us is up

Lesson 112

(Duplicate the test page for each child and fill in the name and date on each test. Be sure each child has a pencil. Distribute the tests.)

1. Put your finger on row 1. Look at the pictures. Which picture shows a dog in a car? Fill in the bubble under the picture of the dog in a car. (Allow time for the students to fill in their answers.) You should have filled in the second bubble. If you did not, cross out your answer and fill in the second bubble now.

2. Touch row 2. Look at the answers. Two of the answers are the same, and one is different. Which answer is different? Fill in the bubble under the answer that is different. (Allow time for the students to fill in their answers.) You should have filled in the first bubble. If you did not, cross out your answer and fill in the first bubble now.

3. Touch row 3. Look at the words. Which word rhymes with **car?** Fill in the bubble under the word that rhymes with **car.** (Allow time for the students to fill in their answers.) You should have filled in the third bubble. If you did not, cross out your answer and fill in the third bubble now.

4. Touch row 4. Look at the answers. Which answer is the word **are?** Fill in the bubble under the word **are.** (Allow time for the students to fill in their answers.) You should have filled in the second bubble. If you did not, cross out your answer and fill in the second bubble now.

It's time to stop. You did a good job filling in the bubbles. **(Collect the test pages.)**

Lesson 112

Name ______________________ Date ______________

1

○ ○ ○

2 th ○ sh ○ sh ○

3 tan ○ tap ○ tar ○

4 and ○ are ○ run ○

(Duplicate the test page for each child and fill in the name and date on each test. Be sure each child has a pencil. Distribute the tests.)

1 Put your finger on row 1. Look at the answers. Which answer makes the sound **ch?** Fill in the bubble under the letter that makes the sound **ch.** (Allow time for the students to fill in their answers.) You should have filled in the third bubble. If you did not, cross out your answer and fill in the third bubble now.

2 Touch row 2. Look at the pictures and words. Which word goes with the picture above it? Fill in the bubble under the word that matches the picture. (Allow time for the students to fill in their answers.) You should have filled in the first bubble. If you did not, cross out your answer and fill in the first bubble now. (**Note:** This is a new item type. If necessary, review with the students how to complete the item.)

3 Touch row 3. Look at the words. Which word rhymes with **art?** Fill in the bubble under the word that rhymes with **art.** (Allow time for the students to fill in their answers.) You should have filled in the second bubble. If you did not, cross out your answer and fill in the second bubble now.

4 Touch row 4. Look at the answers. Which answer is the word **chops?** Fill in the bubble under the word **chops.** (Allow time for the students to fill in their answers.) You should have filled in the third bubble. If you did not, cross out your answer and fill in the third bubble now.

It's time to stop. You did a good job filling in the bubbles. **(Collect the test pages.)**

Lesson 113

Name ______________________ Date ______________

1. th ◯ sh ◯ ch ◯

2.

dog ◯ dog ◯ dog ◯

3. pant ◯ part ◯ path ◯

4. came ◯ cops ◯ chops ◯

Lesson 114

(Duplicate the test page for each child and fill in the name and date on each test. Be sure each child has a pencil. Distribute the tests.)

1. Put your finger on row 1. Look at the pictures. They show a chair, a cake, and a shoe. Which answer begins with the same sound as **chin?** Fill in the bubble under the answer that begins with the same sound as **chin. (Allow time for the students to fill in their answers.)** You should have filled in the first bubble. If you did not, cross out your answer and fill in the first bubble now.

2. Touch row 2. Look at the words. Which word rhymes with **toad?** Fill in the bubble under the word that rhymes with **toad. (Allow time for the students to fill in their answers.)** You should have filled in the third bubble. If you did not, cross out your answer and fill in the third bubble now.

3. Touch row 3. Look at the pictures. Which picture goes with the words *has wheels?* Fill in the bubble under the picture that goes with the words *has wheels.* **(Allow time for the students to fill in their answers.)** You should have filled in the second bubble. If you did not, cross out your answer and fill in the second bubble now.

4. Touch row 4. Look at the answers. Which answer is the word **chips?** Fill in the bubble under the word **chips. (Allow time for the students to fill in their answers.)** You should have filled in the first bubble. If you did not, cross out your answer and fill in the first bubble now.

It's time to stop. You did a good job filling in the bubbles. **(Collect the test pages.)**

Lesson 114

Name ______________________ Date ____________

❶

○ ○ ○

❷ note rake road

○ ○ ○

❸

○ ○ ○

❹ chips hips ships

○ ○ ○

(Duplicate the test page for each child and fill in the name and date on each test. Be sure each child has a pencil. Distribute the tests.)

1. Put your finger on row 1. Look at the words. Which word ends with the sound **ch?** Fill in the bubble under the answer that ends with the sound **ch.** (Allow time for the students to fill in their answers.) You should have filled in the second bubble. If you did not, cross out your answer and fill in the second bubble now.

2. Touch row 2. Look at the pictures. Which picture shows a **cop car?** Fill in the bubble under the picture of the **cop car.** (Allow time for the students to fill in their answers.) You should have filled in the third bubble. If you did not, cross out your answer and fill in the third bubble now.

3. Touch row 3. Look at the words. Two of the words are the same and one is different. Which word is different? Fill in the bubble under the word that is different. (Allow time for the students to fill in their answers.) You should have filled in the second bubble. If you did not, cross out your answer and fill in the second bubble now.

4. Touch row 4. Look at the answers. Which answer is the word **farm?** Fill in the bubble under the word **farm.** (Allow time for the students to fill in their answers.) You should have filled in the first bubble. If you did not, cross out your answer and fill in the first bubble now.

It's time to stop. You did a good job filling in the bubbles. **(Collect the test pages.)**

Lesson 115

Name ______________________ Date ______________

1. eat ○ each ○ ear ○

2. 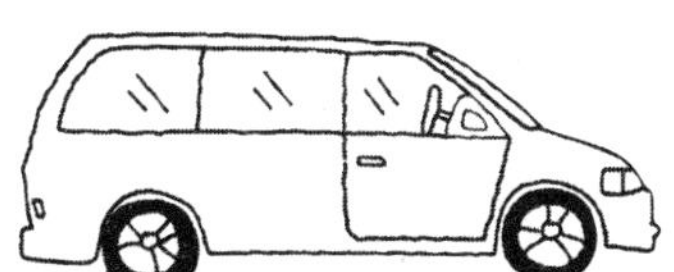 ○ ○  ○

3. or ○ of ○ or ○

4. farm ○ far ○ fish ○

(Duplicate the test page for each child and fill in the name and date on each test. Be sure each child has a pencil. Distribute the tests.)

1. Put your finger on row 1. Look at the pictures. Which picture shows **waves?** Fill in the bubble under the picture of the **waves.** (Allow time for the students to fill in their answers.) You should have filled in the third bubble. If you did not, cross out your answer and fill in the third bubble now.

2. Touch row 2. Look at the words. Which word ends with the sound **lll?** Fill in the bubble under the answer that ends with the sound **lll.** (Allow time for the students to fill in their answers.) You should have filled in the first bubble. If you did not, cross out your answer and fill in the first bubble now.

3. Touch row 3. Look at the pictures and words. Which word goes with the picture above it? Fill in the bubble under the word that matches the picture. (Allow time for the students to fill in their answers.) You should have filled in the second bubble. If you did not, cross out your answer and fill in the second bubble now.

4. Touch row 4. Look at the answers. Which answer is the word **caves?** Fill in the bubble under the word **caves.** (Allow time for the students to fill in their answers.) You should have filled in the second bubble. If you did not, cross out your answer and fill in the second bubble now.

It's time to stop. You did a good job filling in the bubbles. **(Collect the test pages.)**

Lesson 116

Name ____________________ Date ____________

❶

○ ○ ○

❷ will ○ with ○ what ○

❸ girl ○ girl ○ girl ○

❹ cakes ○ caves ○ cars ○

(Duplicate the test page for each child and fill in the name and date on each test. Be sure each child has a pencil. Distribute the tests.)

1. Put your finger on row 1. Look at the pictures. Which picture shows a **cave?** Fill in the bubble under the picture of the **cave.** **(Allow time for the students to fill in their answers.)** You should have filled in the second bubble. If you did not, cross out your answer and fill in the second bubble now.

2. Touch row 2. Look at the answers. Two of the answers are the same, and one is different. Which answer is different? Fill in the bubble under the answer that is different. **(Allow time for the students to fill in their answers.)** You should have filled in the first bubble. If you did not, cross out your answer and fill in the first bubble now.

3. Touch row 3. Look at the pictures. Which picture goes with the words *lives on a farm?* Fill in the bubble under the picture that goes with the words *lives on a farm.* **(Allow time for the students to fill in their answers.)** You should have filled in the third bubble. If you did not, cross out your answer and fill in the third bubble now.

4. Touch row 4. Look at the answers. Which answer is the word **game?** Fill in the bubble under the word **game.** **(Allow time for the students to fill in their answers.)** You should have filled in the first bubble. If you did not, cross out your answer and fill in the first bubble now.

It's time to stop. You did a good job filling in the bubbles. **(Collect the test pages.)**

Lesson 117

Name ______________________ Date ______________

❶

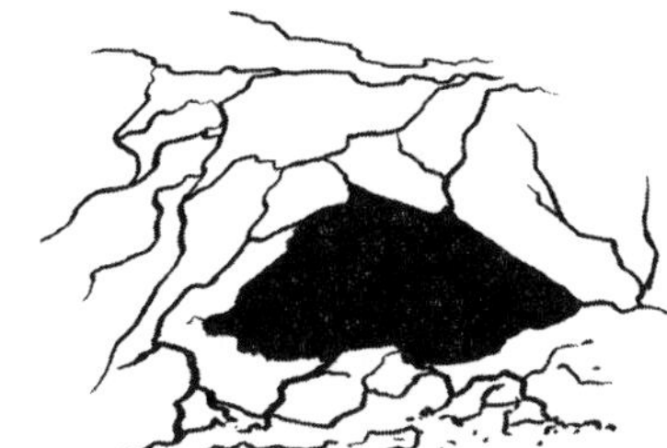

○ ○ ○

❷

p ○ d ○ d ○

❸

○ ○ ○

❹

game ○ safe ○ gave ○

Lesson 118

(Duplicate the test page for each child and fill in the name and date on each test. Be sure each child has a pencil. Distribute the tests.)

1. Put your finger on row 1. Look at the letters. Which letter makes the sound **eee?** Fill in the bubble under the letter that makes the sound **eee. (Allow time for the students to fill in their answers.)** You should have filled in the first bubble. If you did not, cross out your answer and fill in the first bubble now.

2. Touch row 2. Look at the pictures. Which picture shows a pot with no top? Fill in the bubble under the picture of the pot with no top. **(Allow time for the students to fill in their answers.)** You should have filled in the first bubble. If you did not, cross out your answer and fill in the first bubble now.

3. Touch row 3. Look at the answers. Two of the answers are the same, and one is different. Which answer is different? Fill in the bubble under the answer that is different. **(Allow time for the students to fill in their answers.)** You should have filled in the third bubble. If you did not, cross out your answer and fill in the third bubble now.

4. Touch row 4. Look at the answers. Which answer is the word **home?** Fill in the bubble under the word **home. (Allow time for the students to fill in their answers.)** You should have filled in the second bubble. If you did not, cross out your answer and fill in the second bubble now.

It's time to stop. You did a good job filling in the bubbles. **(Collect the test pages.)**

Name ______________________ Date ______________

1 e a l

2 

3 top top tops

4 hose home domes

Lesson 119

(Duplicate the test page for each child and fill in the name and date on each test. Be sure each child has a pencil. Distribute the tests.)

1. Put your finger on row 1. Look at the pictures. Which picture shows **corn?** Fill in the bubble under the picture of **corn. (Allow time for the students to fill in their answers.)** You should have filled in the second bubble. If you did not, cross out your answer and fill in the second bubble now.

2. Touch row 2. Look at the words. Which word begins with the sound **eee?** Fill in the bubble under the answer that begins with the sound **eee. (Allow time for the students to fill in their answers.)** You should have filled in the third bubble. If you did not, cross out your answer and fill in the third bubble now.

3. Touch row 3. Look at the answers. Two of the answers are the same, and one is different. Which answer is different? Fill in the bubble under the answer that is different. **(Allow time for the students to fill in their answers.)** You should have filled in the second bubble. If you did not, cross out your answer and fill in the second bubble now.

4. Touch row 4. Look at the answers. Which answer is the word **lake?** Fill in the bubble under the word **lake. (Allow time for the students to fill in their answers.)** You should have filled in the first bubble. If you did not, cross out your answer and fill in the first bubble now.

It's time to stop. You did a good job filling in the bubbles. **(Collect the test pages.)**

Lesson 119

Name ____________________ Date ____________

❶

○ ○ ○

❷ old ○ ate ○ end ○

❸ her ○ here ○ her ○

❹ lake ○ like ○ take ○

Lesson 120

(Duplicate the test page for each child and fill in the name and date on each test. Be sure each child has a pencil. Distribute the tests.)

Today we are going to do something different. I am going to read a story out loud. Then we will answer some questions about the story. Listen carefully. (Read the story out loud.)

Washing the Car

My sister and I help to wash the car. Mom and dad do most of the work.

We use a bucket of water and a rag. We wipe all the dirt from his car. Then we dry it with another rag.

The last part is the most fun. Dad gives us a special cloth. We rub and rub the car. This makes the car shiny.

Now we will answer the questions.

1. Put your finger on row 1. Look at the pictures. Which picture shows what the story is about? Fill in the bubble under the answer that shows what the story is about. (Allow time for the students to fill in their answers.) You should have filled in the second bubble. If you did not, cross out your answer and fill in the second bubble now.

2. Touch row 2. Look at the pictures. Which picture shows something NOT used in the story? Fill in the bubble under the picture of something NOT used in the story. (Allow time for the students to fill in their answers.) You should have filled in the first bubble. If you did not, cross out your answer and fill in the first bubble now.

It's time to stop. You did a good job filling in the bubbles. Let's go over your answers. **(Review the answers with the children. Collect the test pages.)**

Lesson 120

Name ______________________ Date ______________

1

2

Lesson 121

(Duplicate the test page for each child and fill in the name and date on each test. Be sure each child has a pencil. Distribute the tests.)

1. Put your finger on row 1. Look at the letters. Which letter makes the sound **b?** Fill in the bubble under the letter that makes the sound **b.** **(Allow time for the students to fill in their answers.)** You should have filled in the second bubble. If you did not, cross out your answer and fill in the second bubble now.

2. Touch row 2. Look at the pictures. Which picture goes with the words *something you read?* Fill in the bubble under the picture that goes with the words *something you read.* **(Allow time for the students to fill in their answers.)** You should have filled in the third bubble. If you did not, cross out your answer and fill in the third bubble now.

3. Touch row 3. Look at the words. Which word begins with the sound **p?** Fill in the bubble under the answer that begins with the sound **p.** **(Allow time for the students to fill in their answers.)** You should have filled in the second bubble. If you did not, cross out your answer and fill in the second bubble now.

4. Touch row 4. Look at the answers. Which answer is the word **went?** Fill in the bubble under the word **went.** **(Allow time for the students to fill in their answers.)** You should have filled in the first bubble. If you did not, cross out your answer and fill in the first bubble now.

It's time to stop. You did a good job filling in the bubbles. **(Collect the test pages.)**

Lesson 121

Name ______________________ Date ____________

1 s ◯ b ◯ f ◯

2  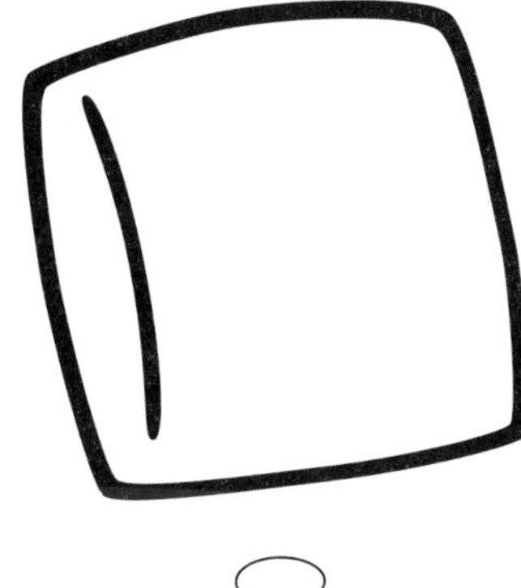 

3 dip ◯ pet ◯ rat ◯

4 went ◯ with ◯ wish ◯

(Duplicate the test page for each child and fill in the name and date on each test. Be sure each child has a pencil. Distribute the tests.)

1. Put your finger on row 1. Look at the letters. Listen carefully. Which letter makes the sound **p?** Fill in the bubble under the letter that makes the sound **p. (Allow time for the students to fill in their answers.)** You should have filled in the third bubble. If you did not, cross out your answer and fill in the third bubble now.

2. Touch row 2. Look at the pictures. Which picture goes with the words *used to paint?* Fill in the bubble under the picture that goes with the words *used to paint.* **(Allow time for the students to fill in their answers.)** You should have filled in the first bubble. If you did not, cross out your answer and fill in the first bubble now.

3. Touch row 3. Look at the answers. Two of the answers are the same, and one is different. Which answer is different? Fill in the bubble under the answer that is different. **(Allow time for the students to fill in their answers.)** You should have filled in the third bubble. If you did not, cross out your answer and fill in the third bubble now.

4. Touch row 4. Look at the answers. Which answer is the word **lift?** Fill in the bubble under the word **lift. (Allow time for the students to fill in their answers.)** You should have filled in the second bubble. If you did not, cross out your answer and fill in the second bubble now.

It's time to stop. You did a good job filling in the bubbles. **(Collect the test pages.)**

Lesson 122

Name ______________________ Date ______________

❶ d ○ b ○ p ○

❷

 ○ ○ 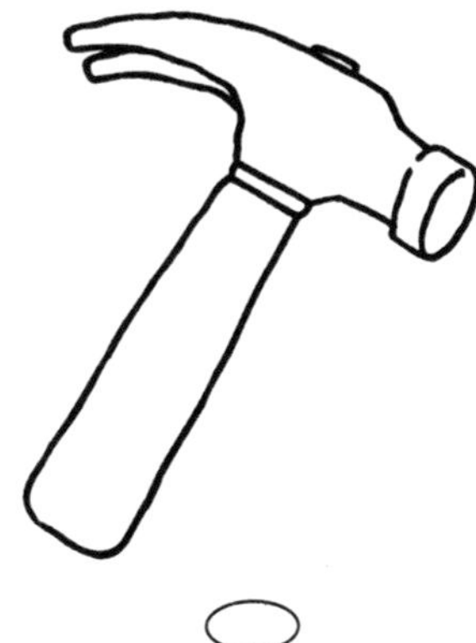 ○

❸ than ○ than ○ then ○

❹ list ○ lift ○ left ○

Lesson 123

(Duplicate the test page for each child and fill in the name and date on each test. Be sure each child has a pencil. Distribute the tests.)

1. Put your finger on row 1. Look at the words. Which word rhymes with **rug?** Fill in the bubble under the word that rhymes with **rug.** (Allow time for the students to fill in their answers.) You should have filled in the first bubble. If you did not, cross out your answer and fill in the first bubble now.

2. Touch row 2. Look at the pictures. Which picture goes with the words *petting a pig?* Fill in the bubble under the picture that goes with the words *petting a pig.* (Allow time for the students to fill in their answers.) You should have filled in the second bubble. If you did not, cross out your answer and fill in the second bubble now.

3. Touch row 3. Look at the pictures and words. Which word goes with the picture above it? Fill in the bubble under the word that matches the picture. (Allow time for the students to fill in their answers.) You should have filled in the third bubble. If you did not, cross out your answer and fill in the third bubble now.

4. Touch row 4. Look at the answers. Which answer is the word **park?** Fill in the bubble under the word **park.** (Allow time for the students to fill in their answers.) You should have filled in the second bubble. If you did not, cross out your answer and fill in the second bubble now.

It's time to stop. You did a good job filling in the bubbles. **(Collect the test pages.)**

Lesson 123

Name ______________________ Date ____________

❶ bug ◯ rat ◯ bed ◯

❷

◯ ◯

◯

❸

chicks ◯ chicks ◯ chicks ◯

❹ dark ◯ park ◯ part ◯

(Duplicate the test page for each child and fill in the name and date on each test. Be sure each child has a pencil. Distribute the tests.)

1. Put your finger on row 1. Look at the answers. Which answer makes the sound **iiing?** Fill in the bubble under the letter that makes the sound **iiing.** (Allow time for the students to fill in their answers.) You should have filled in the first bubble. If you did not, cross out your answer and fill in the first bubble now.

2. Touch row 2. Look at the pictures. Which picture shows someone getting kissed? Fill in the bubble under the picture of the person getting kissed. (Allow time for the students to fill in their answers.) You should have filled in the third bubble. If you did not, cross out your answer and fill in the third bubble now.

3. Touch row 3. Look at the answers. Two of the answers are the same, and one is different. Which answer is different? Fill in the bubble under the answer that is different. (Allow time for the students to fill in their answers.) You should have filled in the second bubble. If you did not, cross out your answer and fill in the second bubble now.

4. Touch row 4. Look at the answers. Which answer is the word **paint?** Fill in the bubble under the word **paint.** (Allow time for the students to fill in their answers.) You should have filled in the first bubble. If you did not, cross out your answer and fill in the first bubble now.

It's time to stop. You did a good job filling in the bubbles. **(Collect the test pages.)**

Lesson 124

Name ______________________ Date ______________

1 ing ◯ ch ◯ th ◯

2  ◯ ◯  ◯

3 these ◯ those ◯ these ◯

4 paint ◯ that ◯ chick ◯

Lesson 125

(Duplicate the test page for each child and fill in the name and date on each test. Be sure each child has a pencil. Distribute the tests.)

1. Put your finger on row 1. Look at the pictures. Which picture goes with the words *someone eating?* Fill in the bubble under the picture that goes with the words *someone eating.* (Allow time for the students to fill in their answers.) You should have filled in the third bubble. If you did not, cross out your answer and fill in the third bubble now.

2. Touch row 2. Look at the answers. Two of the answers are the same, and one is different. Which answer is different? Fill in the bubble under the answer that is different. (Allow time for the students to fill in their answers.) You should have filled in the first bubble. If you did not, cross out your answer and fill in the first bubble now.

3. Touch row 3. Look at the pictures. Which picture shows a **bug?** Fill in the bubble under the picture of the **bug.** (Allow time for the students to fill in their answers.) You should have filled in the second bubble. If you did not, cross out your answer and fill in the second bubble now.

4. Touch row 4. Look at the answers. Which answer is the word **going?** Fill in the bubble under the word **going.** (Allow time for the students to fill in their answers.) You should have filled in the third bubble. If you did not, cross out your answer and fill in the third bubble now.

It's time to stop. You did a good job filling in the bubbles. **(Collect the test pages.)**

Lesson 125

Name ______________________ Date ______________

1  

2 there here here

3   

4 there sleep going

(Duplicate the test page for each child and fill in the name and date on each test. Be sure each child has a pencil. Distribute the tests.)

1. Put your finger on row 1. Look at the words. Which word has the sound **ēēē?** Fill in the bubble under the word that has the sound **ēēē. (Allow time for the students to fill in their answers.)** You should have filled in the second bubble. If you did not, cross out your answer and fill in the second bubble now.

2. Touch row 2. Look at the pictures. Which picture goes with the words *a bug is on the log?* Fill in the bubble under the picture that goes with the words *a bug is on the log.* **(Allow time for the students to fill in their answers.)** You should have filled in the third bubble. If you did not, cross out your answer and fill in the third bubble now.

3. Touch row 3. Look at the answers. Two of the answers are the same, and one is different. Which answer is different? Fill in the bubble under the answer that is different. **(Allow time for the students to fill in their answers.)** You should have filled in the first bubble. If you did not, cross out your answer and fill in the first bubble now.

4. Touch row 4. Look at the answers. Which answer is the word **getting?** Fill in the bubble under the word **getting. (Allow time for the students to fill in their answers.)** You should have filled in the second bubble. If you did not, cross out your answer and fill in the second bubble now.

It's time to stop. You did a good job filling in the bubbles. **(Collect the test pages.)**

Name ______________________________ Date ________________

❶ big ○ be ○ bed ○

❷ 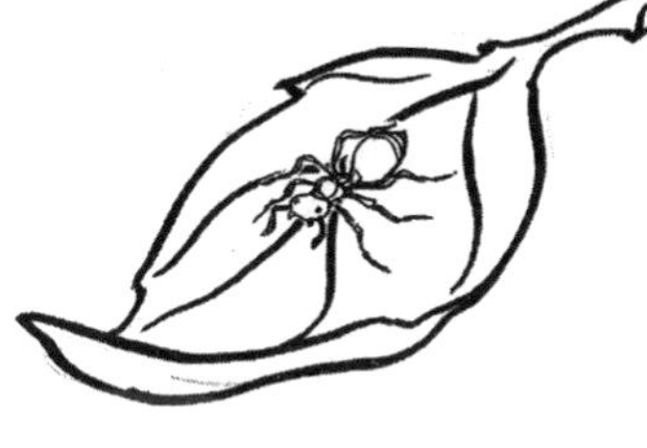 ○ ○  ○

❸ bit ○ hit ○ hit ○

❹ get ○ getting ○ gets ○

(Duplicate the test page for each child and fill in the name and date on each test. Be sure each child has a pencil. Distribute the tests.)

1. Put your finger on row 1. Look at the letters. Which letter makes the sound **īīī?** Fill in the bubble under the letter that makes the sound **īīī. (Allow time for the students to fill in their answers.)** You should have filled in the second bubble. If you did not, cross out your answer and fill in the second bubble now.

2. Touch row 2. Look at the pictures. Which picture goes with the words *someone is fishing?* Fill in the bubble under the picture that goes with the words *someone is fishing.* **(Allow time for the students to fill in their answers.)** You should have filled in the third bubble. If you did not, cross out your answer and fill in the third bubble now.

3. Touch row 3. Look at the pictures and words. Which word goes with the picture above it? Fill in the bubble under the word that matches the picture. **(Allow time for the students to fill in their answers.)** You should have filled in the first bubble. If you did not, cross out your answer and fill in the first bubble now.

4. Touch row 4. Look at the answers. Which answer is the word **sleeping?** Fill in the bubble under the word **sleeping. (Allow time for the students to fill in their answers.)** You should have filled in the second bubble. If you did not, cross out your answer and fill in the second bubble now.

It's time to stop. You did a good job filling in the bubbles. **(Collect the test pages.)**

Name ____________________ Date ____________

1. a ◯ i ◯ e ◯

2.

◯
◯

◯

3.

leaf ◯
leaf ◯

leaf ◯

4. slam ◯ sleeping ◯ going ◯

(Duplicate the test page for each child and fill in the name and date on each test. Be sure each child has a pencil. Distribute the tests.)

1. Put your finger on row 1. Look at the words. Which word has the same beginning sound as **iron?** Fill in the bubble under the answer that has the same beginning sound as **iron.** (Allow time for the students to fill in their answers.) You should have filled in the third bubble. If you did not, cross out your answer and fill in the third bubble now.

2. Touch row 2. Look at the pictures. Which picture shows a **pond?** Fill in the bubble under the picture of the **pond.** (Allow time for the students to fill in their answers.) You should have filled in the second bubble. If you did not, cross out your answer and fill in the second bubble now.

3. Touch row 3. Look at the answers. Two of the answers are the same, and one is different. Which answer is different? Fill in the bubble under the answer that is different. (Allow time for the students to fill in their answers.) You should have filled in the first bubble. If you did not, cross out your answer and fill in the first bubble now.

4. Touch row 4. Look at the answers. Which answer is the word **down?** Fill in the bubble under the word **down.** (Allow time for the students to fill in their answers.) You should have filled in the third bubble. If you did not, cross out your answer and fill in the third bubble now.

It's time to stop. You did a good job filling in the bubbles. **(Collect the test pages.)**

Lesson 128

Name ______________________ Date ______________

1 ant eat ice

2

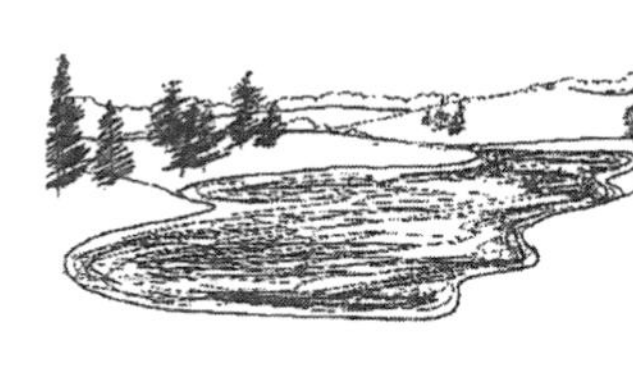

3 walk talk talk

4 kind hand down

(Duplicate the test page for each child and fill in the name and date on each test. Be sure each child has a pencil. Distribute the tests.)

1. Put your finger on row 1. Look at the pictures. Which picture shows a **tub?** Fill in the bubble under the picture of the **tub.** **(Allow time for the students to fill in their answers.)** You should have filled in the first bubble. If you did not, cross out your answer and fill in the first bubble now.

2. Touch row 2. Look at the signs. Which sign says **stop?** Fill in the bubble under the sign that says **stop.** **(Allow time for the students to fill in their answers.)** You should have filled in the second bubble. If you did not, cross out your answer and fill in the second bubble now.

3. Touch row 3. Look at the answers. Two of the answers are the same, and one is different. Which answer is different? Fill in the bubble under the answer that is different. **(Allow time for the students to fill in their answers.)** You should have filled in the third bubble. If you did not, cross out your answer and fill in the third bubble now.

4. Touch row 4. Look at the answers. Which answer is the word **bite?** Fill in the bubble under the word **bite.** **(Allow time for the students to fill in their answers.)** You should have filled in the first bubble. If you did not, cross out your answer and fill in the first bubble now.

It's time to stop. You did a good job filling in the bubbles. **(Collect the test pages.)**

Lesson 129

Name ______________________ Date ______________

1

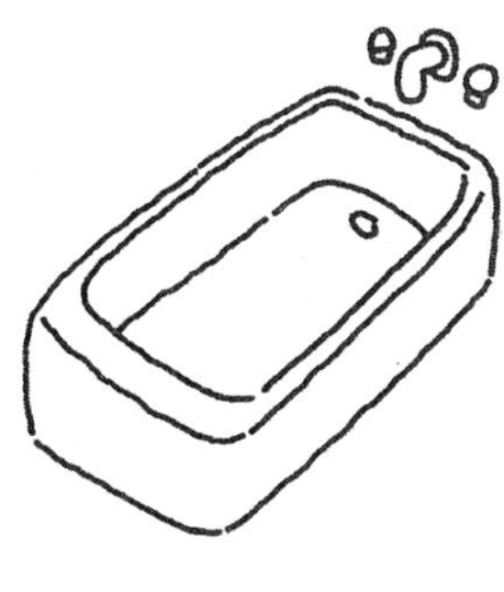

○ ○ ○

2

STOP

○ ○ ○

3 bit ○ bit ○ but ○

4 bite ○ boat ○ meat ○

Lesson 130

(Duplicate the test page for each child and fill in the name and date on each test. Be sure each child has a pencil. Distribute the tests.)

1 Put your finger on row 1. Look at the pictures. Which picture shows someone sliding? Fill in the bubble under the picture of someone sliding. **(Allow time for the students to fill in their answers.)** You should have filled in the second bubble. If you did not, cross out your answer and fill in the second bubble now.

2 Touch row 2. Look at the answers. Which answer shows **lllīīīk?** Fill in the bubble under the answer that shows **lllīīīk. (Allow time for the students to fill in their answers.)** You should have filled in the second bubble. If you did not, cross out your answer and fill in the second bubble now.

3 Touch row 3. Look at the pictures and words. Which word goes with the picture above it? Fill in the bubble under the word that matches the picture. **(Allow time for the students to fill in their answers.)** You should have filled in the third bubble. If you did not, cross out your answer and fill in the third bubble now.

4 Touch row 4. Look at the answers. Which answer is the word **them?** Fill in the bubble under the word **them. (Allow time for the students to fill in their answers.)** You should have filled in the first bubble. If you did not, cross out your answer and fill in the first bubble now.

It's time to stop. You did a good job filling in the bubbles. **(Collect the test pages.)**

Lesson 130

Name ______________________ Date ____________

1

2 bike like line

3

bed bed bed

4 them the that

Lesson 131

(Duplicate the test page for each child and fill in the name and date on each test. Be sure each child has a pencil. Distribute the tests.)

1 Put your finger on row 1. Look at the letters. Which letter makes the first sound you hear in the word **yes**? Fill in the bubble under the letter that makes the first sound in the word **yes**. (Allow time for the students to fill in their answers.) You should have filled in the second bubble. If you did not, cross out your answer and fill in the second bubble now.

2 Touch row 2. Look at the pictures. Which picture shows a **rabbit?** Fill in the bubble under the picture of the **rabbit.** (Allow time for the students to fill in their answers.) You should have filled in the first bubble. If you did not, cross out your answer and fill in the first bubble now.

3 Touch row 3. Look at the answers. Two of the answers are the same, and one is different. Which answer is different? Fill in the bubble under the answer that is different. (Allow time for the students to fill in their answers.) You should have filled in the third bubble. If you did not, cross out your answer and fill in the third bubble now.

4 Touch row 4. Look at the answers. Which answer is the word **more?** Fill in the bubble under the word **more.** (Allow time for the students to fill in their answers.) You should have filled in the first bubble. If you did not, cross out your answer and fill in the first bubble now.

It's time to stop. You did a good job filling in the bubbles. **(Collect the test pages.)**

Lesson 131

Name ______________________ Date ______________

1. a ◯ y ◯ r ◯

2.  ◯ ◯  ◯

3. sleep ◯ sleep ◯ sleeps ◯

4. more ◯ take ◯ with ◯

Lesson 132

(Duplicate the test page for each child and fill in the name and date on each test. Be sure each child has a pencil. Distribute the tests.)

1. Put your finger on row 1. Look at the pictures. Which thing helps you tell time? Fill in the bubble under the picture of something that helps you tell time. **(Allow time for the students to fill in their answers.)** You should have filled in the third bubble. If you did not, cross out your answer and fill in the third bubble now.

2. Touch row 2. Look at the answers. Two of the answers are the same, and one is different. Which answer is different? Fill in the bubble under the answer that is different. **(Allow time for the students to fill in their answers.)** You should have filled in the first bubble. If you did not, cross out your answer and fill in the first bubble now.

3. Touch row 3. Look at the words. Which word ends with the sound **iiing?** Fill in the bubble under the answer that ends with the sound **iiing.** **(Allow time for the students to fill in their answers.)** You should have filled in the second bubble. If you did not, cross out your answer and fill in the second bubble now.

4. Touch row 4. Look at the answers. Which answer is the word **yes?** Fill in the bubble under the word **yes.** **(Allow time for the students to fill in their answers.)** You should have filled in the third bubble. If you did not, cross out your answer and fill in the third bubble now.

It's time to stop. You did a good job filling in the bubbles. **(Collect the test pages.)**

Name ______________________ Date ____________

1

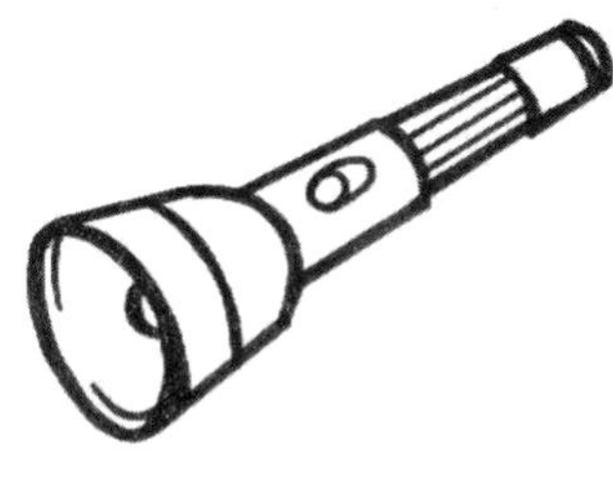

○ ○ ○

2 slide ○ slid ○ slid ○

3 rabbit ○ doing ○ tell ○

4 sit ○ mop ○ yes ○

(Duplicate the test page for each child and fill in the name and date on each test. Be sure each child has a pencil. Distribute the tests.)

1 Put your finger on row 1. Look at the pictures and words. Which word goes with the picture above it? Fill in the bubble under the word that matches the picture. **(Allow time for the students to fill in their answers.)** You should have filled in the first bubble. If you did not, cross out your answer and fill in the first bubble now.

2 Touch row 2. Look at the answers. Two of the answers are the same, and one is different. Which answer is different? Fill in the bubble under the answer that is different. **(Allow time for the students to fill in their answers.)** You should have filled in the second bubble. If you did not, cross out your answer and fill in the second bubble now.

3 Touch row 3. Look at the answers. Which answer shows **bōōōyyy?** Fill in the bubble under the answer that shows **bōōōyyy. (Allow time for the students to fill in their answers.)** You should have filled in the third bubble. If you did not, cross out your answer and fill in the third bubble now.

4 Touch row 4. Look at the answers. Which answer is the word **into?** Fill in the bubble under the word **into. (Allow time for the students to fill in their answers.)** You should have filled in the second bubble. If you did not, cross out your answer and fill in the second bubble now.

It's time to stop. You did a good job filling in the bubbles. **(Collect the test pages.)**

Lesson 133

Name ______________________ Date ______________

1. park ◯ park ◯ park ◯

2. led ◯ red ◯ led ◯

3. park ◯ you ◯ boy ◯

4. not ◯ into ◯ ton ◯

Lesson 134

(Duplicate the test page for each child and fill in the name and date on each test. Be sure each child has a pencil. Distribute the tests.)

1. Put your finger on row 1. Look at the pictures. Which picture shows someone digging? Fill in the bubble under the picture of someone digging. **(Allow time for the students to fill in their answers.)** You should have filled in the third bubble. If you did not, cross out your answer and fill in the third bubble now.

2. Touch row 2. Look at the answers. Two of the answers are the same, and one is different. Which answer is different? Fill in the bubble under the answer that is different. **(Allow time for the students to fill in their answers.)** You should have filled in the second bubble. If you did not, cross out your answer and fill in the second bubble now.

3. Touch row 3. Look at the pictures. Which picture shows a **hole?** Fill in the bubble under the picture of the **hole.** **(Allow time for the students to fill in their answers.)** You should have filled in the first bubble. If you did not, cross out your answer and fill in the first bubble now.

4. Touch row 4. Look at the answers. Which answer is the word **lived?** Fill in the bubble under the word **lived.** **(Allow time for the students to fill in their answers.)** You should have filled in the third bubble. If you did not, cross out your answer and fill in the third bubble now.

It's time to stop. You did a good job filling in the bubbles. **(Collect the test pages.)**

Lesson 134

Name ______________________ Date ______________

1

○ ○ ○

2

yes ○

you ○

yes ○

3

○ ○ ○

4

liked ○

line ○

lived ○

(Duplicate the test page for each child and fill in the name and date on each test. Be sure each child has a pencil. Distribute the tests.)

1 Put your finger on row 1. Look at the answers. Which answer shows **errrrrr?** Fill in the bubble under the answer that shows **errrrrr.** (Allow time for the students to fill in their answers.) You should have filled in the second bubble. If you did not, cross out your answer and fill in the second bubble now.

2 Touch row 2. Look at the pictures. Which picture goes with the words *paint the bed?* Fill in the bubble under the picture that goes with the words *paint the bed.* (Allow time for the students to fill in their answers.) You should have filled in the third bubble. If you did not, cross out your answer and fill in the third bubble now.

3 Touch row 3. Look at the words. Which word has the same middle sound as **top?** Fill in the bubble under the answer that has the same middle sound as **top.** (Allow time for the students to fill in their answers.) You should have filled in the second bubble. If you did not, cross out your answer and fill in the second bubble now.

4 Touch row 4. Look at the answers. Which answer is the word **find?** Fill in the bubble under the word **find.** (Allow time for the students to fill in their answers.) You should have filled in the first bubble. If you did not, cross out your answer and fill in the first bubble now.

It's time to stop. You did a good job filling in the bubbles. **(Collect the test pages.)**

Lesson 135

Name ______________________ Date ______________

1 en ◯ er ◯ ev ◯

2  ◯ ◯ 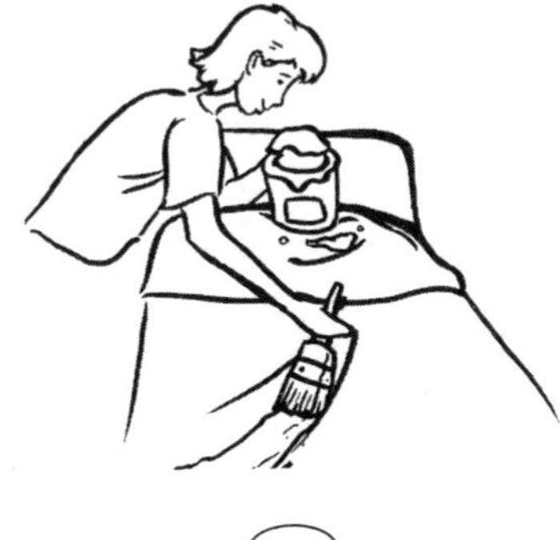 ◯

3 bed ◯ mom ◯ dad ◯

4 find ◯ fin ◯ fish ◯

(Duplicate the test page for each child and fill in the name and date on each test. Be sure each child has a pencil. Distribute the tests.)

1. Put your finger on row 1. Look at the answers. Two of the answers are the same, and one is different. Which answer is different? Fill in the bubble under the answer that is different. (Allow time for the students to fill in their answers.) You should have filled in the first bubble. If you did not, cross out your answer and fill in the first bubble now.

2. Touch row 2. Look at the pictures. Which picture goes with the words *something you ride?* Fill in the bubble under the picture that goes with the words *something you ride.* (Allow time for the students to fill in their answers.) You should have filled in the third bubble. If you did not, cross out your answer and fill in the third bubble now.

3. Touch row 3. Look at the words. Which word rhymes with **near?** Fill in the bubble under the word that rhymes with **near.** (Allow time for the students to fill in their answers.) You should have filled in the first bubble. If you did not, cross out your answer and fill in the first bubble now.

4. Touch row 4. Look at the answers. Which answer is the word **hunt?** Fill in the bubble under the word **hunt.** (Allow time for the students to fill in their answers.) You should have filled in the second bubble. If you did not, cross out your answer and fill in the second bubble now.

It's time to stop. You did a good job filling in the bubbles. **(Collect the test pages.)**

Lesson 136

Name ______________________ Date ______________

❶ er ◯ e ◯ e ◯

❷  ◯ ◯  ◯

❸ here ◯ walk ◯ slid ◯

❹ run ◯ hunt ◯ hat ◯

(Duplicate the test page for each child and fill in the name and date on each test. Be sure each child has a pencil. Distribute the tests.)

1. Put your finger on row 1. Look at the pictures. Which picture shows a **deer?** Fill in the bubble under the picture of the **deer.** **(Allow time for the students to fill in their answers.)** You should have filled in the third bubble. If you did not, cross out your answer and fill in the third bubble now.

2. Touch row 2. Look at the words. Two of the words are the same and one is different. Which word is different? Fill in the bubble under the word that is different. **(Allow time for the students to fill in their answers.)** You should have filled in the second bubble. If you did not, cross out your answer and fill in the second bubble now.

3. Touch row 3. Look at the answers. Which answer shows **sssēēēnnn?** Fill in the bubble under the answer that shows **sssēēēnnn.** **(Allow time for the students to fill in their answers.)** You should have filled in the third bubble. If you did not, cross out your answer and fill in the third bubble now.

4. Touch row 4. Look at the answers. Which answer is the word **love?** Fill in the bubble under the word **love.** **(Allow time for the students to fill in their answers.)** You should have filled in the first bubble. If you did not, cross out your answer and fill in the first bubble now.

It's time to stop. You did a good job filling in the bubbles. **(Collect the test pages.)**

Lesson 137

Name ______________________ Date ______________

1

2 brother mother brother

3 near sit seen

4 love that slip

(Duplicate the test page for each child and fill in the name and date on each test. Be sure each child has a pencil. Distribute the tests.)

1. Put your finger on row 1. Look at the answers. Two of the answers are the same, and one is different. Which answer is different? Fill in the bubble under the answer that is different. **(Allow time for the students to fill in their answers.)** You should have filled in the third bubble. If you did not, cross out your answer and fill in the third bubble now.

2. Touch row 2. Look at the pictures. Which picture goes with the words *birthday card?* Fill in the bubble under the picture that goes with the words *birthday card.* **(Allow time for the students to fill in their answers.)** You should have filled in the first bubble. If you did not, cross out your answer and fill in the first bubble now.

3. Touch row 3. Look at the answers. Which answer shows **her?** Fill in the bubble under the answer that shows **her. (Allow time for the students to fill in their answers.)** You should have filled in the second bubble. If you did not, cross out your answer and fill in the second bubble now.

4. Touch row 4. Look at the answers. Which answer is the word **other?** Fill in the bubble under the word **other. (Allow time for the students to fill in their answers.)** You should have filled in the third bubble. If you did not, cross out your answer and fill in the third bubble now.

It's time to stop. You did a good job filling in the bubbles. **(Collect the test pages.)**

Lesson 138

Name ______________________ Date ______________

1 gave ◯ gave ◯ give ◯

2  ◯ ◯  

3 him ◯ her ◯ his ◯

4 not ◯ her ◯ other ◯

(Duplicate the test page for each child and fill in the name and date on each test. Be sure each child has a pencil. Distribute the tests.)

1. Put your finger on row 1. Look at the pictures. Which picture goes with the words *grocery shopping?* Fill in the bubble under the picture that goes with the words *grocery shopping.* **(Allow time for the students to fill in their answers.)** You should have filled in the second bubble. If you did not, cross out your answer and fill in the second bubble now.

2. Touch row 2. Look at the words. Two of the words are the same and one is different. Which word is different? Fill in the bubble under the word that is different. **(Allow time for the students to fill in their answers.)** You should have filled in the third bubble. If you did not, cross out your answer and fill in the third bubble now.

3. Touch row 3. Look at the words. Which word ends with the sound **errr?** Fill in the bubble under the answer that ends with the sound **errr.** **(Allow time for the students to fill in their answers.)** You should have filled in the first bubble. If you did not, cross out your answer and fill in the first bubble now.

4. Touch row 4. Look at the answers. Which answer is the word **never?** Fill in the bubble under the word **never.** **(Allow time for the students to fill in their answers.)** You should have filled in the first bubble. If you did not, cross out your answer and fill in the first bubble now.

It's time to stop. You did a good job filling in the bubbles. **(Collect the test pages.)**

Lesson 139

Name ______________________ Date ______________

1  ◯  ◯  ◯

2 boys ◯ boys ◯ toys ◯

3 other ◯ beans ◯ going ◯

4 never ◯ sent ◯ rear ◯

(Duplicate the test page for each child and fill in the name and date on each test. Be sure each child has a pencil. Distribute the tests.)

Today we are going to do something different. I am going to read a story out loud. Then we will answer some questions about the story. Listen carefully. (Read the story out loud.)

Waiting

Nick was a sad dog. He was home with Mom. The children were in school. He missed Ella and Eddie.

All day, Nick sat by the door. After a while, he heard voices. Next he heard footsteps. Then he heard the door open. Ella and Eddie were home.

Nick wagged his tail. Ella and Eddie petted him. They said hi to Mom. Then they went outside with Nick. He was a happy dog.

Now we will answer the questions.

1. Put your finger on row 1. Look at the pictures. Which picture shows what animal is in the story? Fill in the bubble under the answer that shows what animal is in the story. (Allow time for the students to fill in their answers.) You should have filled in the third bubble. If you did not, cross out your answer and fill in the third bubble now.

2. Touch row 2. Look at the pictures. Which picture shows where Nick waited? Fill in the bubble under the picture that shows where Nick waited. (Allow time for the students to fill in their answers.) You should have filled in the third bubble. If you did not, cross out your answer and fill in the third bubble now.

It's time to stop. You did a good job filling in the bubbles. Let's go over your answers. **(Review the answers with the children. Collect the test pages.)**

Lesson 140

Name ______________________ Date ______________

1

2

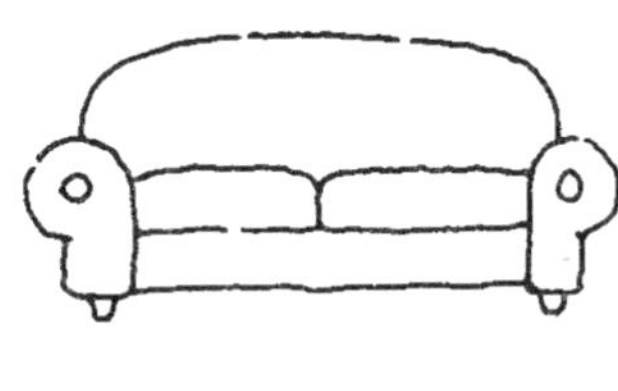

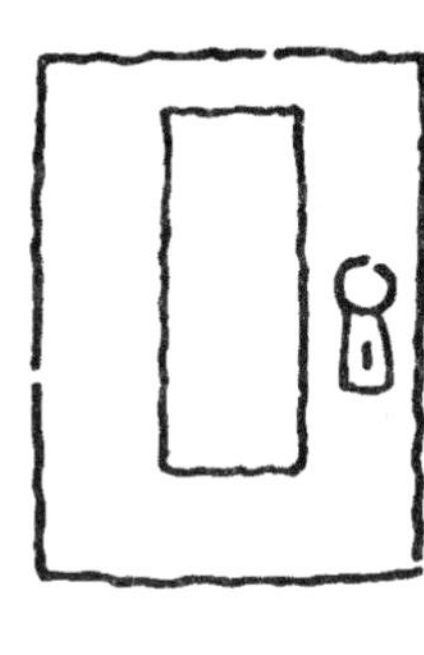

(Duplicate the test page for each child and fill in the name and date on each test. Be sure each child has a pencil. Distribute the tests.)

1. Put your finger on row 1. Look at the letters. Which letter makes the last sound you hear in the word **box?** Fill in the bubble under the letter that makes the last sound in the word **box. (Allow time for the students to fill in their answers.)** You should have filled in the second bubble. If you did not, cross out your answer and fill in the second bubble now.

2. Touch row 2. Look at the pictures. Which picture shows a **fox?** Fill in the bubble under the picture of the **fox. (Allow time for the students to fill in their answers.)** You should have filled in the third bubble. If you did not, cross out your answer and fill in the third bubble now.

3. Touch row 3. Look at the pictures. Which picture goes with the words *little toy duck?* Fill in the bubble under the picture that goes with the words *little toy duck.* **(Allow time for the students to fill in their answers.)** You should have filled in the first bubble. If you did not, cross out your answer and fill in the first bubble now.

4. Touch row 4. Look at the answers. Which answer is the word **come?** Fill in the bubble under the word **come. (Allow time for the students to fill in their answers.)** You should have filled in the second bubble. If you did not, cross out your answer and fill in the second bubble now.

It's time to stop. You did a good job filling in the bubbles. **(Collect the test pages.)**

Lesson 141

Name ______________________ Date ______________

1

r ◯ x ◯ m ◯

2

 ◯

 ◯

 ◯

3

 ◯

 ◯

 ◯

4

hop ◯ come ◯ toys ◯

(Duplicate the test page for each child and fill in the name and date on each test. Be sure each child has a pencil. Distribute the tests.)

1. Put your finger on row 1. Look at the pictures. Which picture shows an **eagle?** Fill in the bubble under the picture of the **eagle.** **(Allow time for the students to fill in their answers.)** You should have filled in the third bubble. If you did not, cross out your answer and fill in the third bubble now.

2. Touch row 2. Look at the answer. Which letters make the middle sound you hear in the word **moon**? Fill in the bubble under the letters that make the middle sound in the word **moon**. **(Allow time for the students to fill in their answers.)** You should have filled in the first bubble. If you did not, cross out your answer and fill in the first bubble now.

3. Touch row 3. Look at the pictures. Which picture goes with the words *hitting a ball?* Fill in the bubble under the picture that goes with the words *hitting a ball.* **(Allow time for the students to fill in their answers.)** You should have filled in the second bubble. If you did not, cross out your answer and fill in the second bubble now.

4. Touch row 4. Look at the answers. Which answer is the word **ever?** Fill in the bubble under the word **ever.** **(Allow time for the students to fill in their answers.)** You should have filled in the third bubble. If you did not, cross out your answer and fill in the third bubble now.

It's time to stop. You did a good job filling in the bubbles. **(Collect the test pages.)**

Lesson 142

Name ______________________ Date ______________

1

2 oo aa ee

3

4 sent talk ever

(Duplicate the test page for each child and fill in the name and date on each test. Be sure each child has a pencil. Distribute the tests.)

1. Put your finger on row 1. Look at the pictures. Which picture goes with the words *a wet animal?* Fill in the bubble under the picture that goes with the words *a wet animal.* (Allow time for the students to fill in their answers.) You should have filled in the first bubble. If you did not, cross out your answer and fill in the first bubble now.

2. Touch row 2. Look at the answers. Which answer shows **yyyooouuu?** Fill in the bubble under the answer that shows **yyyooouuu.** (Allow time for the students to fill in their answers.) You should have filled in the third bubble. If you did not, cross out your answer and fill in the third bubble now.

3. Touch row 3. Look at the answers. Two of the answers are the same, and one is different. Which answer is different? Fill in the bubble under the answer that is different. (Allow time for the students to fill in their answers.) You should have filled in the first bubble. If you did not, cross out your answer and fill in the first bubble now.

4. Touch row 4. Look at the answers. Which answer is the word **shore?** Fill in the bubble under the word **shore.** (Allow time for the students to fill in their answers.) You should have filled in the second bubble. If you did not, cross out your answer and fill in the second bubble now.

It's time to stop. You did a good job filling in the bubbles. **(Collect the test pages.)**

Lesson 143

Name ______________________ Date ______________

1

○ ○ ○

2 the ○ yes ○ you ○

3 slide ○ slider ○ slider ○

4 there ○ shore ○ those ○

Lesson 144

(Duplicate the test page for each child and fill in the name and date on each test. Be sure each child has a pencil. Distribute the tests.)

1. Put your finger on row 1. Look at the words. Which word has the same middle sound as **soon?** Fill in the bubble under the answer that has the same middle sound as **soon.** **(Allow time for the students to fill in their answers.)** You should have filled in the third bubble. If you did not, cross out your answer and fill in the third bubble now.

2. Touch row 2. Look at the pictures. Which picture shows a **dime?** Fill in the bubble under the picture of the **dime.** **(Allow time for the students to fill in their answers.)** You should have filled in the third bubble. If you did not, cross out your answer and fill in the third bubble now.

3. Touch row 3. Look at the words. Two of the words are the same and one is different. Which word is different? Fill in the bubble under the word that is different. **(Allow time for the students to fill in their answers.)** You should have filled in the second bubble. If you did not, cross out your answer and fill in the second bubble now.

4. Touch row 4. Look at the answers. Which answer is the word **sitting?** Fill in the bubble under the word **sitting.** **(Allow time for the students to fill in their answers.)** You should have filled in the first bubble. If you did not, cross out your answer and fill in the first bubble now.

It's time to stop. You did a good job filling in the bubbles. **(Collect the test pages.)**

Lesson 144

Name ______________________ Date ______________

❶ fish ◯ paint ◯ broom ◯

❷

❸ chore ◯ shore ◯ chore ◯

❹ sitting ◯ girl ◯ ever ◯

(Duplicate the test page for each child and fill in the name and date on each test. Be sure each child has a pencil. Distribute the tests.)

1. Put your finger on row 1. Look at the letters. Which letter makes the first sound you hear in the word **jump?** Fill in the bubble under the letter that makes the first sound in the word **jump.** (Allow time for the students to fill in their answers.) You should have filled in the second bubble. If you did not, cross out your answer and fill in the second bubble now.

2. Touch row 2. Look at the pictures. Which picture goes with the words *a pile of dirt?* Fill in the bubble under the picture that goes with the words *a pile of dirt.* (Allow time for the students to fill in their answers.) You should have filled in the first bubble. If you did not, cross out your answer and fill in the first bubble now.

3. Touch row 3. Look at the words. Two of the words are the same and one is different. Which word is different? Fill in the bubble under the word that is different. (Allow time for the students to fill in their answers.) You should have filled in the third bubble. If you did not, cross out your answer and fill in the third bubble now.

4. Touch row 4. Look at the answers. Which answer is the word **chip?** Fill in the bubble under the word **chip.** (Allow time for the students to fill in their answers.) You should have filled in the first bubble. If you did not, cross out your answer and fill in the first bubble now.

It's time to stop. You did a good job filling in the bubbles. **(Collect the test pages.)**

Lesson 145

Name ______________________ Date ______________

1 p ○ j ○ t ○

2

○ ○ ○

3 than ○ than ○ then ○

4 chip ○ moon ○ then ○

Lesson 146

(Duplicate the test page for each child and fill in the name and date on each test. Be sure each child has a pencil. Distribute the tests.)

1. Put your finger on row 1. Look at the pictures. Which picture shows a **brush?** Fill in the bubble under the picture of the **brush.** **(Allow time for the students to fill in their answers.)** You should have filled in the second bubble. If you did not, cross out your answer and fill in the second bubble now.

2. Touch row 2. Look at the answers. Two of the answers are the same, and one is different. Which answer is different? Fill in the bubble under the answer that is different. **(Allow time for the students to fill in their answers.)** You should have filled in the first bubble. If you did not, cross out your answer and fill in the first bubble now.

3. Touch row 3. Look at the letters. Which letter makes the sound **juuh?** Fill in the bubble under the letter that makes the sound **juuh.** **(Allow time for the students to fill in their answers.)** You should have filled in the second bubble. If you did not, cross out your answer and fill in the second bubble now.

4. Touch row 4. Look at the answers. Which answer is the word **must?** Fill in the bubble under the word **must.** **(Allow time for the students to fill in their answers.)** You should have filled in the third bubble. If you did not, cross out your answer and fill in the third bubble now.

It's time to stop. You did a good job filling in the bubbles. **(Collect the test pages.)**

Lesson 146

Name ______________________ Date ______________

1

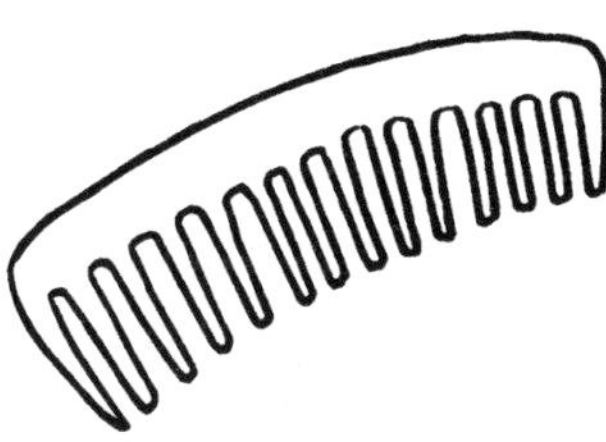

○ ○ ○

2 walked ○ walk ○ walk ○

3 h ○ j ○ d ○

4 will ○ farm ○ must ○

Lesson 147

(Duplicate the test page for each child and fill in the name and date on each test. Be sure each child has a pencil. Distribute the tests.)

1. Put your finger on row 1. Look at the pictures. Which picture shows a **pool?** Fill in the bubble under the picture of the **pool. (Allow time for the students to fill in their answers.)** You should have filled in the first bubble. If you did not, cross out your answer and fill in the first bubble now.

2. Touch row 2. Look at the words. Which word has the sound **vvv?** Fill in the bubble under the answer that has the sound **vvv. (Allow time for the students to fill in their answers.)** You should have filled in the third bubble. If you did not, cross out your answer and fill in the third bubble now.

3. Touch row 3. Look at the answers. Two of the answers are the same, and one is different. Which answer is different? Fill in the bubble under the answer that is different. **(Allow time for the students to fill in their answers.)** You should have filled in the first bubble. If you did not, cross out your answer and fill in the first bubble now.

4. Touch row 4. Look at the answers. Which answer is the word **jump?** Fill in the bubble under the word **jump. (Allow time for the students to fill in their answers.)** You should have filled in the second bubble. If you did not, cross out your answer and fill in the second bubble now.

It's time to stop. You did a good job filling in the bubbles. **(Collect the test pages.)**

Lesson
147

Name ______________________ Date ______________

❶

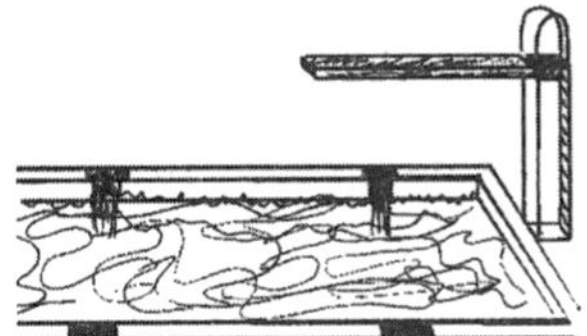

○ ○ ○

❷ walked ○ either ○ never ○

❸ them ○ they ○ they ○

❹ must ○ jump ○ tore ○

(Duplicate the test page for each child and fill in the name and date on each test. Be sure each child has a pencil. Distribute the tests.)

1 Put your finger on row 1. Look at the pictures. Which picture shows the **moon?** Fill in the bubble under the picture of the **moon.** (Allow time for the students to fill in their answers.) You should have filled in the first bubble. If you did not, cross out your answer and fill in the first bubble now.

2 Touch row 2. Look at the words. Two of the words are the same and one is different. Which word is different? Fill in the bubble under the word that is different. (Allow time for the students to fill in their answers.) You should have filled in the second bubble. If you did not, cross out your answer and fill in the second bubble now.

3 Touch row 3. Look at the words. Which word has the same middle sound as **home?** Fill in the bubble under the answer that has the same middle sound as **home.** (Allow time for the students to fill in their answers.) You should have filled in the first bubble. If you did not, cross out your answer and fill in the first bubble now.

4 Touch row 4. Look at the answers. Which answer is the word **some?** Fill in the bubble under the word **some.** (Allow time for the students to fill in their answers.) You should have filled in the third bubble. If you did not, cross out your answer and fill in the third bubble now.

It's time to stop. You did a good job filling in the bubbles. **(Collect the test pages.)**

Name ______________________ Date ______________

1

2 jump jumps jump

3 broke will sent

4 pool soon some

Lesson 149

(Duplicate the test page for each child and fill in the name and date on each test. Be sure each child has a pencil. Distribute the tests.)

1. Put your finger on row 1. Look at the letters. Which letter makes the sound **yyy?** Fill in the bubble under the letter that makes the sound **yyy.** **(Allow time for the students to fill in their answers.)** You should have filled in the second bubble. If you did not, cross out your answer and fill in the second bubble now.

2. Touch row 2. Look at the words. Two of the words are the same and one is different. Which word is different? Fill in the bubble under the word that is different. **(Allow time for the students to fill in their answers.)** You should have filled in the third bubble. If you did not, cross out your answer and fill in the third bubble now.

3. Touch row 3. Look at the pictures. Which picture goes with the words *an animal that jumps?* Fill in the bubble under the picture that goes with the words *an animal that jumps.* **(Allow time for the students to fill in their answers.)** You should have filled in the first bubble. If you did not, cross out your answer and fill in the first bubble now.

4. Touch row 4. Look at the answers. Which answer is the word **says?** Fill in the bubble under the word **says.** **(Allow time for the students to fill in their answers.)** You should have filled in the second bubble. If you did not, cross out your answer and fill in the second bubble now.

It's time to stop. You did a good job filling in the bubbles. **(Collect the test pages.)**

Lesson 149

Name ______________________ Date ______________

1. j ◯ y ◯ h ◯

2. bring ◯ bring ◯ bringing ◯

3.  ◯ ◯ 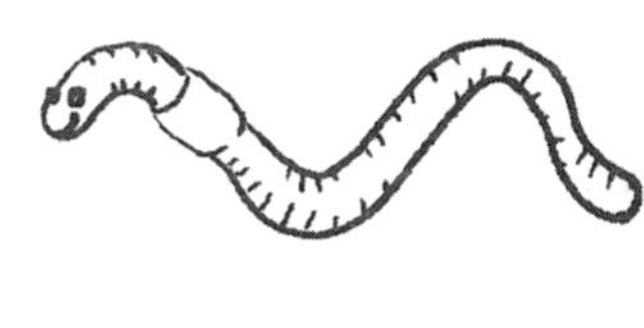 ◯

4. chip ◯ says ◯ wet ◯

(Duplicate the test page for each child and fill in the name and date on each test. Be sure each child has a pencil. Distribute the tests.)

1. Put your finger on row 1. Look at the pictures. Which picture shows a **barn?** Fill in the bubble under the picture of the **barn. (Allow time for the students to fill in their answers.)** You should have filled in the first bubble. If you did not, cross out your answer and fill in the first bubble now.

2. Touch row 2. Look at the words. Two of the words are the same and one is different. Which word is different? Fill in the bubble under the word that is different. **(Allow time for the students to fill in their answers.)** You should have filled in the first bubble. If you did not, cross out your answer and fill in the first bubble now.

3. Touch row 3. Look at the pictures. Which picture goes with the words *an animal you ride?* Fill in the bubble under the picture that goes with the words *an animal you ride.* **(Allow time for the students to fill in their answers.)** You should have filled in the second bubble. If you did not, cross out your answer and fill in the second bubble now.

4. Touch row 4. Look at the answers. Which answer is the word **other?** Fill in the bubble under the word **other. (Allow time for the students to fill in their answers.)** You should have filled in the third bubble. If you did not, cross out your answer and fill in the third bubble now.

It's time to stop. You did a good job filling in the bubbles. **(Collect the test pages.)**

Name ____________________ Date ____________

❶

○ ○ ○

❷ get ○ got ○ got ○

❸

○ ○ ○

❹ riding ○ talked ○ other ○

Lesson 151

(Duplicate the test page for each child and fill in the name and date on each test. Be sure each child has a pencil. Distribute the tests.)

1. Put your finger on row 1. Look at the pictures. Which picture goes with the words *tug on the rope?* Fill in the bubble under the picture that goes with the words *tug on the rope.* (Allow time for the students to fill in their answers.) You should have filled in the third bubble. If you did not, cross out your answer and fill in the third bubble now.

2. Touch row 2. Look at the answers. Two of the answers are the same, and one is different. Which answer is different? Fill in the bubble under the answer that is different. (Allow time for the students to fill in their answers.) You should have filled in the third bubble. If you did not, cross out your answer and fill in the third bubble now.

3. Touch row 3. Look at the pictures and words. Which word does not go with the picture above it? Fill in the bubble under the word that does not match the picture. (Allow time for the students to fill in their answers.) You should have filled in the second bubble. If you did not, cross out your answer and fill in the second bubble now.

4. Touch row 4. Look at the answers. Which answer is the word **fine?** Fill in the bubble under the word **fine.** (Allow time for the students to fill in their answers.) You should have filled in the second bubble. If you did not, cross out your answer and fill in the second bubble now.

It's time to stop. You did a good job filling in the bubbles. **(Collect the test pages.)**

Name ____________________ Date ____________

❶

❷ teacher teacher teach

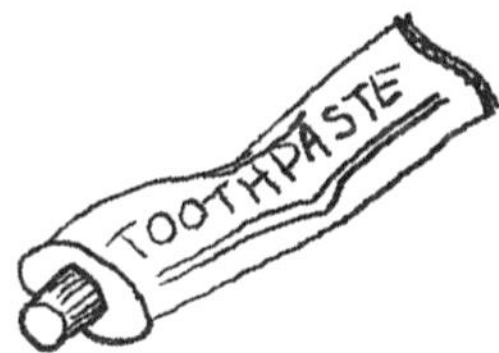

❸ brush brush brush

❹ nine fine fire

(Duplicate the test page for each child and fill in the name and date on each test. Be sure each child has a pencil. Distribute the tests.)

1. Put your finger on row 1. Look at the pictures and words. Which word goes with the picture above it? Fill in the bubble under the word that matches the picture. **(Allow time for the students to fill in their answers.)** You should have filled in the second bubble. If you did not, cross out your answer and fill in the second bubble now.

2. Touch row 2. Look at the letters. Which letters make the first sound you hear in the word **why?** Fill in the bubble under the letters that make the first sound in the word **why. (Allow time for the students to fill in their answers.)** You should have filled in the third bubble. If you did not, cross out your answer and fill in the third bubble now.

3. Touch row 3. Look at the answers. Which answer shows **ffflllȳȳȳ?** Fill in the bubble under the answer that shows **ffflllȳȳȳ. (Allow time for the students to fill in their answers.)** You should have filled in the first bubble. If you did not, cross out your answer and fill in the first bubble now.

4. Touch row 4. Look at the answers. Which answer is the word **your?** Fill in the bubble under the word **your. (Allow time for the students to fill in their answers.)** You should have filled in the third bubble. If you did not, cross out your answer and fill in the third bubble now.

It's time to stop. You did a good job filling in the bubbles. **(Collect the test pages.)**

Lesson 152

Name ____________________ Date ____________

❶

book	book	book
◯	◯	◯

❷

th	ch	wh
◯	◯	◯

❸

fly	my	fox
◯	◯	◯

❹

says	you	your
◯	◯	◯

(Duplicate the test page for each child and fill in the name and date on each test. Be sure each child has a pencil. Distribute the tests.)

1. Put your finger on row 1. Look at the pictures. Which picture goes with the words *I like to fly?* Fill in the bubble under the picture that goes with the words *I like to fly.* (Allow time for the students to fill in their answers.) You should have filled in the first bubble. If you did not, cross out your answer and fill in the first bubble now.

2. Touch row 2. Look at the words. Two of the words are the same and one is different. Which word is different? Fill in the bubble under the word that is different. (Allow time for the students to fill in their answers.) You should have filled in the second bubble. If you did not, cross out your answer and fill in the second bubble now.

3. Touch row 3. Look at the answers. Which answer is a number word? Fill in the bubble under the number word. (Allow time for the students to fill in their answers.) You should have filled in the third bubble. If you did not, cross out your answer and fill in the third bubble now.

4. Touch row 4. Look at the answers. Which answer is the word **into?** Fill in the bubble under the word **into.** (Allow time for the students to fill in their answers.) You should have filled in the second bubble. If you did not, cross out your answer and fill in the second bubble now.

It's time to stop. You did a good job filling in the bubbles. **(Collect the test pages.)**

Lesson 153

Name ______________________ Date ______________

1  

2 look book look

3 are cop six

4 went into barn

(Duplicate the test page for each child and fill in the name and date on each test. Be sure each child has a pencil. Distribute the tests.)

1 Put your finger on row 1. Look at the letters. Which letters make the first sound you hear in the word **quick?** Fill in the bubble under the letters that make the first sound in the word **quick. (Allow time for the students to fill in their answers.)** You should have filled in the third bubble. If you did not, cross out your answer and fill in the third bubble now.

2 Touch row 2. Look at the words. Two of the words are the same and one is different. Which word is different? Fill in the bubble under the word that is different. **(Allow time for the students to fill in their answers.)** You should have filled in the second bubble. If you did not, cross out your answer and fill in the second bubble now.

3 Touch row 3. Look at the pictures. Which picture shows **teeth?** Fill in the bubble under the picture of the **teeth. (Allow time for the students to fill in their answers.)** You should have filled in the first bubble. If you did not, cross out your answer and fill in the first bubble now.

4 Touch row 4. Look at the answers. Which answer is the word **where?** Fill in the bubble under the word **where. (Allow time for the students to fill in their answers.)** You should have filled in the third bubble. If you did not, cross out your answer and fill in the third bubble now.

It's time to stop. You did a good job filling in the bubbles. **(Collect the test pages.)**

Lesson 154

Name ______________________ Date ______________

❶ ch ◯ wh ◯ qu ◯

❷ time ◯ times ◯ time ◯

❸  ◯  ◯ ◯

❹ here ◯ white ◯ where ◯

(Duplicate the test page for each child and fill in the name and date on each test. Be sure each child has a pencil. Distribute the tests.)

1. Put your finger on row 1. Look at the pictures. Which picture goes with the words *brush your teeth?* Fill in the bubble under the picture that goes with the words *brush your teeth.* (Allow time for the students to fill in their answers.) You should have filled in the second bubble. If you did not, cross out your answer and fill in the second bubble now.

2. Touch row 2. Look at the words. Two of the words are the same and one is different. Which word is different? Fill in the bubble under the word that is different. (Allow time for the students to fill in their answers.) You should have filled in the third bubble. If you did not, cross out your answer and fill in the third bubble now.

3. Touch row 3. Look at the words. Which word rhymes with **much?** Fill in the bubble under the word that rhymes with **much.** (Allow time for the students to fill in their answers.) You should have filled in the second bubble. If you did not, cross out your answer and fill in the second bubble now.

4. Touch row 4. Look at the answers. Which answer is the word **why?** Fill in the bubble under the word **why.** (Allow time for the students to fill in their answers.) You should have filled in the first bubble. If you did not, cross out your answer and fill in the first bubble now.

It's time to stop. You did a good job filling in the bubbles. **(Collect the test pages.)**

Lesson 155

Name ______________________ Date ______________

❶

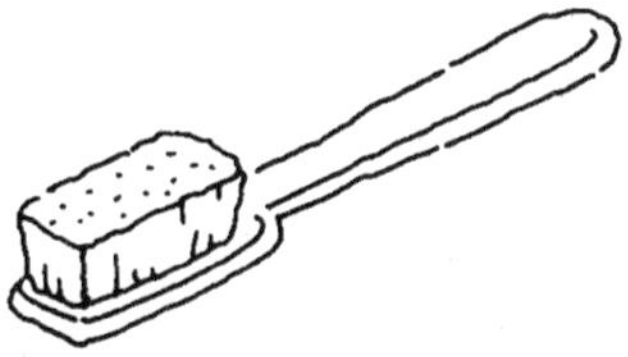

○ ○ ○

❷ smile ○ smile ○ smiled ○

❸ shine ○ touch ○ white ○

❹ why ○ my ○ fly ○

(Duplicate the test page for each child and fill in the name and date on each test. Be sure each child has a pencil. Distribute the tests.)

1 Put your finger on row 1. Look at the letters. Which letter makes the first sound you hear in the word **zoo?** Fill in the bubble under the letter that makes the first sound in the word **zoo.** (Allow time for the students to fill in their answers.) You should have filled in the first bubble. If you did not, cross out your answer and fill in the first bubble now.

2 Touch row 2. Look at the pictures and words. Which word goes with the picture above it? Fill in the bubble under the word that matches the picture. (Allow time for the students to fill in their answers.) You should have filled in the first bubble. If you did not, cross out your answer and fill in the first bubble now.

3 Touch row 3. Look at the words. Two of the words are the same and one is different. Which word is different? Fill in the bubble under the word that is different. (Allow time for the students to fill in their answers.) You should have filled in the third bubble. If you did not, cross out your answer and fill in the third bubble now.

4 Touch row 4. Look at the answers. Which answer is the word **where?** Fill in the bubble under the word **where.** (Allow time for the students to fill in their answers.) You should have filled in the second bubble. If you did not, cross out your answer and fill in the second bubble now.

It's time to stop. You did a good job filling in the bubbles. **(Collect the test pages.)**

Lesson 156

Name ______________________ Date ______________

1. z ◯ x ◯ v ◯

2.

tree ◯ tree ◯ tree ◯

3. under ◯ under ◯ after ◯

4. when ◯ where ◯ there ◯

Lesson 157

(Duplicate the test page for each child and fill in the name and date on each test. Be sure each child has a pencil. Distribute the tests.)

1 Put your finger on row 1. Look at the pictures. Which picture goes with the words *a fast animal?* Fill in the bubble under the picture that goes with the words *a fast animal.* (Allow time for the students to fill in their answers.) You should have filled in the third bubble. If you did not, cross out your answer and fill in the third bubble now.

2 Touch row 2. Look at the words. Which word has the most letters? Fill in the bubble under the word with the most letters. (Allow time for the students to fill in their answers.) You should have filled in the second bubble. If you did not, cross out your answer and fill in the second bubble now.

3 Touch row 3. Look at the pictures. Which picture shows a **tiger?** Fill in the bubble under the picture of the **tiger.** (Allow time for the students to fill in their answers.) You should have filled in the third bubble. If you did not, cross out your answer and fill in the third bubble now.

4 Touch row 4. Look at the answers. Which answer is the word **under?** Fill in the bubble under the word **under.** (Allow time for the students to fill in their answers.) You should have filled in the first bubble. If you did not, cross out your answer and fill in the first bubble now.

It's time to stop. You did a good job filling in the bubbles. **(Collect the test pages.)**

Name ______________________ Date ______________

1

○ ○ ○

2 fast ○ teeth ○ why ○

3

○ ○ ○

4 under ○ teeth ○ things ○

(Duplicate the test page for each child and fill in the name and date on each test. Be sure each child has a pencil. Distribute the tests.)

1. Put your finger on row 1. Look at the pictures and words. Which word goes with the picture above it? Fill in the bubble under the word that matches the picture. **(Allow time for the students to fill in their answers.)** You should have filled in the first bubble. If you did not, cross out your answer and fill in the first bubble now.

2. Touch row 2. Look at the words. Which word begins with the sound **ōōō?** Fill in the bubble under the answer that begins with the sound **ōōō.** **(Allow time for the students to fill in their answers.)** You should have filled in the second bubble. If you did not, cross out your answer and fill in the second bubble now.

3. Touch row 3. Look at the words. Two of the words are the same and one is different. Which word is different? Fill in the bubble under the word that is different. **(Allow time for the students to fill in their answers.)** You should have filled in the second bubble. If you did not, cross out your answer and fill in the second bubble now.

4. Touch row 4. Look at the answers. Which answer is the word **thing?** Fill in the bubble under the word **thing.** **(Allow time for the students to fill in their answers.)** You should have filled in the third bubble. If you did not, cross out your answer and fill in the third bubble now.

It's time to stop. You did a good job filling in the bubbles. **(Collect the test pages.)**

Name ______________________ Date ______________

1

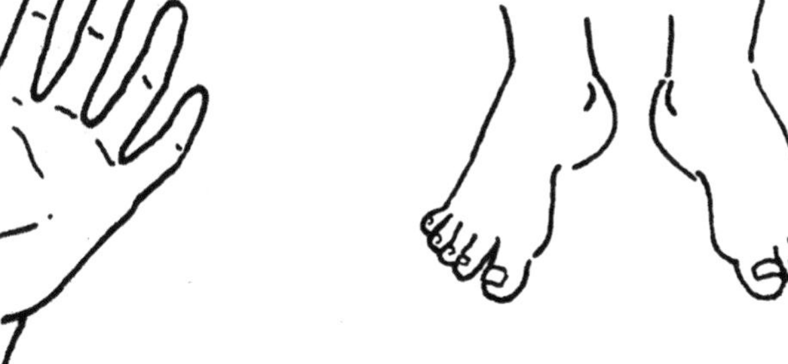

head	head	head
○	○	○

2

under	over	after
○	○	○

3

life	wife	life
○	○	○

4

show	took	thing
○	○	○

(Duplicate the test page for each child and fill in the name and date on each test. Be sure each child has a pencil. Distribute the tests.)

1 Put your finger on row 1. Look at the pictures. Which picture shows a **pie?** Fill in the bubble under the picture of the **pie.** (Allow time for the students to fill in their answers.) You should have filled in the second bubble. If you did not, cross out your answer and fill in the second bubble now.

2 Touch row 2. Look at the words. Two of the words are the same and one is different. Which word is different? Fill in the bubble under the word that is different. (Allow time for the students to fill in their answers.) You should have filled in the third bubble. If you did not, cross out your answer and fill in the third bubble now.

3 Touch row 3. Look at the words. Which word rhymes with **last?** Fill in the bubble under the word that rhymes with **last.** (Allow time for the students to fill in their answers.) You should have filled in the first bubble. If you did not, cross out your answer and fill in the first bubble now.

4 Touch row 4. Look at the answers. Which answer is the word **even?** Fill in the bubble under the word **even.** (Allow time for the students to fill in their answers.) You should have filled in the second bubble. If you did not, cross out your answer and fill in the second bubble now.

It's time to stop. You did a good job filling in the bubbles. **(Collect the test pages.)**

Lesson 159

Name ______________________ Date ______________

1
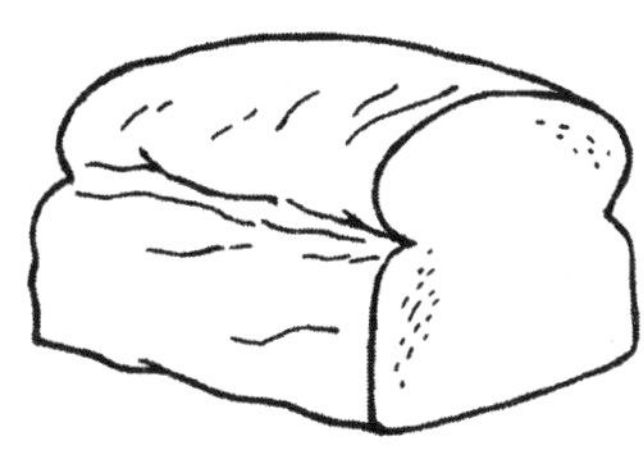

2 wipe wipe wife

3 fast fell tell

4 went even bent

Lesson 160

(Duplicate the test page for each child and fill in the name and date on each test. Be sure each child has a pencil. Distribute the tests.)

Today we are going to do something different. I am going to read a story out loud. Then we will answer some questions about the story. Listen carefully. (Read the story out loud.)

The Wind

The wind does many things. It blows clouds across the sky. It moves the leaves on the trees.

I like to fly a kite in the wind. The kite goes high in the sky. If the wind stops, the kite comes down.

Sometimes the wind blows hard. It can blow dust around. If the wind blows very hard, it can knock down trees.

Now we will answer the questions.

1 Put your finger on row 1. Look at the pictures. Which toy is in the story? Fill in the bubble under the picture of the toy in the story. (Allow time for the students to fill in their answers.) You should have filled in the first bubble. If you did not, cross out your answer and fill in the first bubble now.

2 Touch row 2. Look at the pictures. What does the story say a strong wind can blow down? Fill in the bubble under the picture of something the story says the wind can blow down. (Allow time for the students to fill in their answers.) You should have filled in the third bubble. If you did not, cross out your answer and fill in the third bubble now.

It's time to stop. You did a good job filling in the bubbles. Let's go over your answers. **(Review the answers with the children. Collect the test pages.)**

Name ______________________________ Date ____________________

❶

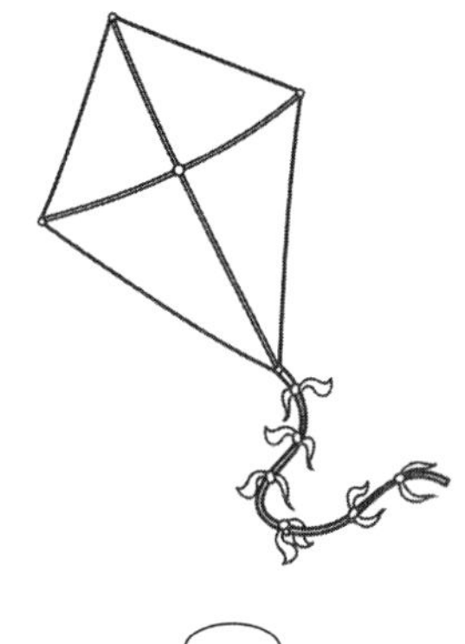

❷